It Happens Only in India

R.N. Sharma

PEACOCK BOOKS

Published by
PEACOCK BOOKS
7/22, Ansari Road, Darya Ganj,
New Delhi-110002
Phones : +91-11-40775252, 23273880, 23275880, 23280451
Fax : +91-11-23285873
Web : www.atlanticbooks.com
E-mail : orders@atlanticbooks.com

Branch Office
5, Nallathambi Street, Wallajah Road,
Chennai-600002
Phones : +91-44-64611085, 32413319
E-mail : chennai@atlanticbooks.com

Peacock Books is an imprint of
Atlantic Publishers and Distributors (P) Ltd

ISBN 978-81-248-0250-2

Printed in India at Nice Printing Press, A-33/3A, Site-IV,
Industrial Area, Sahibabad, Ghaziabad, U.P.

PREFACE

This book contains some of the very interesting and readable pieces published in different newspapers starting from 1980 (earlier it was only an on and off affair) when my first piece was carried by the *The Tribune* of Chandigarh, and I owe that success to late Mr. Prem Bhatia, the then Editor-in-Chief of the paper.

I had met Mr. Bhatia (for less than three minutes) in the Tribune's Bureau Office in New Delhi and showed him the piece which was not accepted for publication earlier. He just glanced through it, patted me and said, "I assure you it will go into print." The meeting and the pat gave me much-needed confidence and encouragement and there was no looking back for me. I must have written more than three hundred pieces after that, most of which were published.

I must also thank Mr. T.N. Nair (I have never met him) of *Hindustan Times*, who through his 'notes' on the margins of some of my pieces, had guided me in his own way.

Finally, I owe my thanks to Mr. Manish Gupta, Managing Director, Atlantic Publishers and Distributors (P) Ltd. for considering and accepting my proposal to publish these pieces in a book form.

The collection is not dated and can provide some moments of joy and food for thought to the readers.

I would like to dedicate the book to my late wife, Usha, who always encouraged and inspired me in my writing work. I owe much to her.

R.N. Sharma

CONTENTS

1

A MATTER OF ADDRESS

I continue to maintain an old tradition and address my wife as "Mein kiha ji" (please listen to what I say). That is how my elders have been and are addressing their spouses.

However, my uncles prefer to address their wives after the names of their first children, for example, as "Prabha-ki-Mata" or "Shashi-ki-Mummy". I do not know how they managed before they were blessed with their firstborns. Perhaps that was a period of sweet nothings and the language of love sufficed.

My wife has been critical of me for not addressing her by name. She holds the view that couples who address each other by name are more informal and intimate. Well, it is not true of our neighbours and one or two of my cousins. If shouting and abuse are informality, I am not willing to opt for it.

But even if my wife's suggestion were to be accepted, the use of the name will remain the privilege of the husband. The better halves will remain orthodox, despite the constitutional guarantee of equality of the sexes and all this noise about women's lib.

I know of couples who address each other by shortening the first name. The wife, for instance, addresses her husband as "Ran"—short for Ranbir—and the husband "Ani"—short for Anita. And there are some who manage with just "yaar".

There are some couples who have acquired an imported form. They address each other as "Honey". But what can one make of these "Honeys" when they argue in anger? I once overheard the following dialogue:

"Honey don't be stupid."

"You are talking rubbish, Honey."

Then there are wives who use initials to address or refer to their husbands. For example, "D.P." for Dharam Pal.

There are some brides who carry their nicknames to the husbands' houses. "Romy" continues to be "Romy" and does not change to Madhu for her husband.

However, I recently ran into a classic example of Indo-Anglian culture when a couple who had migrated to the U.K. about a decade ago paid a visit to us. They addressed each other in a very unusual manner:

Wife: "Darling ji zara sunanaa".

Husband: "Bolo Madam ji".

2

A FADING MEMORY

It was an instant decision on the eve of Gandhi Jayanti celebrations that prompted me to go to Raj Ghat.

I got up early humming "Ram Dhun". My wife cried out: "Allow us to sleep at least on a holiday". I toned down my voice.

A bus for Raj Ghat was my next target. I was at the bus stop well before six. But there was no bus for the next 45 minutes. I wondered how people in large numbers managed to reach Raj Ghat on time for the prayers.

Then came a mini bus. It was full, but I managed to get in. Some more people got in at the next stop. It was suffocating inside, and I requested the conductor not to allow more passengers to come in. He shouted at me and asked me not to teach him his job. That silenced me.

Another passenger, guessing my embarrassment, said: "We travel in these mini buses because others are not available. Majboori ka naam Mahatma Gandhi hai". I could not understand how the Mahatma came into the picture.

We reached Raj Ghat. There were more policemen and other officials than ordinary citizens. A crowd of 500 people stood on one side of the *samadhi*—all in immaculate spotless khadi and looking fresh. When I compared my dishevelled condition with them I felt sure that they had not travelled by bus.

The VIPs started arriving and that started hectic activity. Some of those present stretched their necks over the heads of the VIPs to catch the eye of the cameras.

A prayer meeting followed. Hymns from the scriptures of different religions were sung, but all in a half-hearted manner. Some in the gathering were getting restless.

The VIPs started leaving. It took another 10 minutes for the others to melt away.

Some two dozen enthusiasts were still spinning on the charkhas. How long would they continue? I was not sure.

I visited Gandhi Smarak Nidhi. Not more than 20 people were present and most of them were past 80.

I visited the Gandhi Mela. It was a real mela—chaat stalls, swings, games of skill—more than anything Gandhian.

As I was returning home by another bus one of the passengers asked: "Why do they declare a national holiday on October 2? Do we celebrate birthdays with closed bazaars? The day is not far off when October 2 will not be a national holiday."

I looked back. The words had come from the mouth of a young man in a T-shirt and jeans.

As a finale to the day. I played a Subbulakshmi cassette of the favourite bhajans of Gandhiji. The children were upset and wanted me to reduce the volume or use the ear-phone.

3

HINDUSTAN HAMARA

Muthuswamy from Madras is of the firm opinion that national integration is not possible till the Hindi chauvinists do not stop telling the Tamilians to learn Hindi.

When told that film producers from the South are themselves encouraging Hindi by making Hindi movies, he criticises them for dancing to the tune of Hindiwallas in order to make quick bucks.

He takes to task the producer of a popular Hindi movie for making hero (who falls in love with a girl from the North) learn Hindi. Could not the producer do the other way round? he asks.

Amarjit Singh, back from a visit to Amritsar, is a sad man. He is perturbed over the popularity of dosa, vada, sambar and idli, in a place known for 'makki ki roti', 'sarson ka saag' and 'dahi ki lassi'. He had been touring South but did not find South Indians patronizing the 'dabbas' serving Punjabi dishes. It is a clear-cut case of dietetical dominance of South over North, he argues.

Bhomkar from Bombay is in high spirit these days. He is grateful to the Shiv Sena for reviving the 'sons of the soil' slogan.

Mallayya from Mysore is also happy with Kannada cine actor Raj Kumar for striving to give a pride of place to Kannada in Karnataka.

Chatterjee from Calcutta, residing in Delhi for the last 30 years, is very often heard saying that his head and heart lie in Calcutta only. He often muses "Aamar Sonar Bangla Desh".

Barua from Bongaigaon takes exception to his colleague. Majumdar's claim that he belongs to Assam. He is a foreigner, he argues.

Ganga Ram from Gorakhpur speaks angrily of the Union Industries Minister for ignoring his own state. When reminded about the oil refinery at Mathura and the Indian Telephone Industries unit at Naini, he gets agitated. They are in western region of the state, he tells us.

Panikkar from Palghat is more concerned about the happenings in the Gulf countries than what is happening in Kashmir Valley. That state is in the north-most tip of the country, he informs us.

But above all, comes the chorus being sung by the school children at the Republic Day parade. They still sing "Sare Jahan Se Achcha Hindustan Hamara".

4

A DIMINISHING WANT

It seems to me that the craze for calendars which is at its feverish peak in the first week of each new year, is on the wane. Immediate evidence lies in the fact that this year I have not been pestered for calendars and diaries as in the past. Being in the publishing profession, I am always approached for these annual gifts.

Among my calendar hunting friends is a colleague who always asked for three calendars. Until he explained the reason for this numerical preference, I always wondered why he wanted three, and not two or one.

His reply was: "One for the kitchen to help my wife record the supply of the milk received in the house; second for the bed room and the third for the living room."

A one-sheet calendar was good enough for the kitchen but it should indicate the Vikrami dates and festivals like Purnima (full moon night), Amavasya (no moon night) etc. The one for the bed-room should be functional, giving details of government and bank holidays. But the one for the living room had to be beautiful. This one could be a six-sheeter or even bigger. Thus, his demand for calendars was always utility-based.

In December 1983, I expected him to place his usual indent with me. But he did not, although we had been meeting almost every day.

As he did not come forward with his annual request for the first two days of the new year, I got really perplexed. For a moment I thought he was obsessed with George Orwell's 1984 and would not like to be reminded daily that he was going through the fateful year. But he confessed that he had not even heard of this piece of fiction.

"Don't you need your quota of calendars this year?" I asked him.

"No. I don't need three this year", he said with a grin. "However if you can spare one, that will do."

"Only one?"

"Yes. In November last year I shifted to a one-room apartment with a make-shift kitchen of wooden planks and an asbestos sheet roof."

I wondered whether he would need next year even the one calendar he wanted for 1984.

5

POINT OF NO RETURN

I stood glaring at the 'House Full' sign outside a cinema hall. And I would have stood on trying to destroy the obstacle with my Third Eye, when a familiar voice whispered in my ear: 'Sahib, ticket?' I turned back to find—who but Ramu, in a soiled T-shirt and faded jeans, chewing paan and puffing at a cigarette. Almost a smuggler's sidekick straight out of a Hindi film.

He had changed a lot. He was not the boy I had known two years ago. From a scrawny shoeshine boy, he had grown into something of a muscleman.

Though I was not his regular customer, I had noticed the quiet lad so unlike his peers in the profession boy on the pavement, and made friends with him.

Then one day he had disappeared, to be seen again only now. I had asked some of his friends about him and was told that he had left the brush-and-polish business.

'Sahib, you'? He was surprised to see me.

I asked him what had happened to him and his story would have sounded *filmi* if one did not know it was sordidly real-life.

He would have continued the shoeshine work, he said, but for 'Lala', outside whose shop he used to sit. "Once he involved me in a theft case, there was no peace for me. For any pickpocketing, eve-teasing or theft case, the police used to haul me up, though they let me off after a day or two. I was fed up".

But the frequent visits to the thana had taught him all the tricks of cop-tackling, and "now they do not bother me any more".

"But why should Lala have involved you in the theft case at all?"

"He wanted me to vacate the spot to expand his shop. I pleaded with him again and again and I was even willing to pay more rent for the spot, but he would not relent."

He talked like a *dada* with a fair sprinkling of obscenities.

I wanted to tell him to return to his old trade or take up some other honest work. But he had no time to listen to me.

"I have still two tickets for his show. I must sell them and return for the next show", he said and melted into the crowd.

I wondered whether he had not reached a point of no return.

6

A NEW PARTY IS BORN

Taking my cue from our seasoned and veteran politicians, I have also decided to float a party. In my school and college days, I indulged in plenty of "partybazi" and can beat most of my countrymen at the game.

My party, when formed, will be suited to Indian political conditions and leaders.

I have tentatively decided to name it "Bharatiya Desam Sarvadharma Dalit Janata Mazdoor Samajwad Janwad Kazhagam... ( )". The dots will come in handy if any further groups or splinters decide to merge. The blank parenthesis will be used as a suffix in case of a split.

The party will be "broad-based" and persons of any "zaat" and "paat" can seek membership. Any "topiwala", "dhotiwala" and "haisiyatwala" (Indian equivalents for Tom, Dick and Harry) can join the party.

The party will not have any constitution, thereby avoiding the need for interpreting it.

To avoid any misunderstanding arising from colour preference, the party will have a rainbow on its flag.

To avoid possible rivalries among the leaders (there will be only leaders but no cadres and workers), the party will not have any office-bearers like President, Working President or General Secretary.

A multi-faced human being, almost resembling Ravana, will be the election symbol.

Lest the party should be accused of being Leftist, Rightist or even Centrist, it will not have any programmes and policies. To escape unfair criticism by the people and the Press, it will be free from any activity. Day-to-day point programmes will be announced, thereby keeping the Opposition in complete suspense.

As discipline breeds dissidence in our country, no effort will be made to enforce any discipline. All the leaders will have the right to criticize the party and fellow leaders.

Keeping in view the best traditions of Indian political life, the party members will have the complete freedom to split and resplit the party, and if not successful, the splitter will have every right to come back to the parent organization.

As with all other political parties in the country, the sole aim of BDSDJMSJK... ( ) will be to fight elections and grab power by hook or by crook.

7

HAIRDO FASHIONS

We are told that the Prime Minister Rajiv Gandhi had a particular barber to cut his hair. So do I. I have been to the same barber for some 15 years. They say that approved barbers and tailors should not be changed.

But the man who handles my head is not as privileged as the one whose saloon was visited by the Prime Minister. Since the Prime Minister is a Very Important Person, the barbar is a Very Privileged Person. The first label does not fit me, nor does the second fit my hair cutter.

The latter has recently revised his tarrif. This is the third revision in the current calendar year ordered by Khan Sahib who cuts only gentlemen's hair, although he does occasionally accommodate accompanying children.

"I hate cutting children's hair", he told me once. "I can manage three men within the time spent on a child."

What really attracted my attention in the new tariff was the addition of a new item. This is called "stylish cutting" for which the cost is an additional five rupees.

In my school days some of the boys insisted on the "Dilip Kumar style" (this was soon after the release of his film, *Mela*). None of them looked anything like the matinee idol.

I tried to pattern my hairstyle after Dev Anand, but that again was uncalled for.

"Sadhana cut" (Sadhana used that pattern in *Mere Mehboob*) was as popular as the "Dilip Kumar style" and it was a craze with young girls. This was sometimes against the wishes of their parents.

To come back to "stylish cutting", I asked Khan Sahib: "What is this stylish cutting?"

"This is meant for customers who insist on having a particular style or are fussy," he replied. "You are different. You leave everything to me."

"What is the popular style these days?" I enquired and answered the question myself: "Must be that of Amitabh Bachchan".

"Forget Amitabh Bachchan", said the barber. "Everybody these days—young and old—insists on a small crop."

This was how Rajiv Gandhi liked to have his hair cut.

8

THE WORLD OF PAPERBAGS

When somebody asked me in Washington what visible changes had come about in India, I replied that the vegetable sellers and *pakora-wallas* were doing away with paperbags and packing their stuff in polythene bags. Now it is a matter of prestige for a shopkeeper to supply things in polythene bags, and at least some customers display these like trophies.

For the affluent America, this change may not seen to be of any significance, but for us Indians it certainly is a sign of progress.

But, personally speaking, I can only grieve over the unceremonious exit of the paperbags. They used to offer a varied fare—casual reading sometimes, educative material, now and then, and rarely even something to ponder over.

I still remember to have read the banned short story (it was carried by a Hindi journal) "Sardarji" by K.A. Abbas only from paperbags where it was keeping company with potatoes and onions.

A still from K. Asifs "Hulchul' which showed Raj Kapoor kissing Nargis (the scene was deleted from the film later), was found on a paperbag handed over by a fruit-vendor.

I remember an elderly person in our neighbourhood, who used to get annoyed with shopkeepers who sold their stuff in paperbags bearing pictures of gods and goddesses, which many other cherished. Lest the deities were shown any disrespect, he very often paid for such paperbags and made special arrangements to get them immersed in the Yamuna.

But the most depressing aspect of the change from paper to polythene bag is the slump that has come about in the *kabadi* market. Whether newspaper printed on imported newsprint or journals done on glazed art paper, the *kabadiwala* is quoting less and less every time he is offered the wastepaper.

"There is no market for paper now", we are told.

Probably the day is not very far off when the newspapers and journals will be thrown into garbage bins as is being done in America. Converted into paperbags as of old, how much less ephemeral would the printed word and picture have been!

But I am certain with environmentalists raising their voice against the use of polythene bags, the paperbags are sure to stage a comeback.

9

THE SNORING SYNDROME

One wonders what prompted the Japanese doctors to go all the way to England, and that too Hampshire, to find a man who snores. They are experimenting on him to know the whys and whats of snoring.

But why did the Japanese have to go thousands of miles to get a snoring man when they could have found a good number of the snoring species nearer East, or right under their nose?

Many in India must be feeling envious of the gentleman from Hampshire who has snored his way to Tokyo.

Had there been an open world competition (with a lure of world gold cup) we would have been the champions?

What is snoring? Nothing but some noisy and harsh sounds that emanate during sleep through one's mouth or mouth and nose both, with the soft palate playing the key role.

There are snorers who whistle in high and low tones. Some snore rhythmically and some in uneven tones. Certain individuals produce coughing sounds.

Then there are those who snore only in the beginning of their sleep and stop snoring after some time. However, there are some who snore in the last hours of their sleep.

Whatever be the snoring sound and time, it is one aspect of a person's life, which an individual is not in a position to judge for himself or herself. It is the others who make comments, mostly with sarcasm and in a lighter vein.

I know of a lady who every night shifts to the children's bedroom because she is not able to stand the snoring of her husband. Had she been in the US or some other country of the West, she might by now have divorced the man.

The most disgusting situation is when a person snores while you are talking something sweet or serious.

A snoring guest is another nuisance, especially if you are sharing the room with him or her. Recently we had a guest who snored all night, making all sorts of peculiar sounds and kept us awake.

In the morning he complained that he had not had good sleep!

May be the myth whether a person who snores sleep well or not will be clear after the Japanese have experimented on the gentleman from Hampshire.

However, a colleague informs that those who snuff their noses during the day do not snore in the night. But this information has been provided by one who is a snuff addict. Only one who lies (not sleeps) by the side of his bed can confirm it.

This piece will not be complete unless I append a personal note.

I was all the time under the impression that I do not snore until recently my wife told me that I do, though the sounds are feeble and mild.

Isn't a case of snoring in whispers?

Another case study for the Japanese experts to experiment with.

10

AN INTELLECTUALS' WORKSHOP

More than the subject of discussion at the workshop it was the venue that really interested me. This was one of the five-star hotels of the Capital. The thought of going to the hotel cheered me up.

Once at the hotel, my first job was to get myself registered. The lady who took down my particulars handed over to me a portfolio containing a few cyclostyled sheets of paper, a brochure and a ball pen. Another lady pinned a badge on my coat.

The preliminaries over, we were taken into the workshop in the banquet hall. But the Minister who was to inaugurate the function was half an hour late. His arrival was heralded by the clicking of cameras and the flashing of lights (for the benefit of the television cameramen).

The workshop organizers crowded by the side of the Minister to catch the eye of the camera.

We started the proceedings with the welcome address. The organizers expressed their gratitude to the Minister for sparing some of his valuable time in the midst of a very busy schedule. (I was sure he had no other work on that day because he did not seem to be in a hurry to leave).

The Minister formally declared the workshop open by delivering a sermon on what should be done by intellectuals (I an "intellectual"? I felt flattered) to solve the country's problems. Although the Minister said nothing profound, one of the organizers who spoke after him was sure that the workshop would be immensely benefited by the views of the Minister.

Soon the coffee break was announced and everyone rushed to the lobbies. As usual, several persons came forward to prepare cups of coffee for their bosses and stood by for any further demands on their services.

A Secretary in the Central Government quietly asked one of his aides to take the staff car to his residence. (His wife was to go shopping.)

The workshop started immediately after the coffee break. We were asked to take out from our portfolios our copies of the keynote address specially prepared for the workshop.

We listened to the address with studied patience, but a few in the audience went out and some never came back. Two ladies kept up their gossip session, an elderly gentleman went to sleep, a few doodled or played with their ball pens and some busied themselves in correcting their copies. There was a constant sound of crockery being removed or placed, which was a prelude to the lunch break.

After lunch the attendance became very thin for the discussion session. We were asked to raise queries, but few asked any questions. I was certain that many in the audience had not understood what had been said in the keynote paper. But many got up to congratulate the author of the paper.

The tea break was announced, and there was again a rush on the tea tables. A group photograph was taken after the break.

We assembled for the final session to get the rapporteur's concluding remarks. He repeated what we had already heard.

One of the participants thanked the Chairman and the organizers for the excellent arrangements. (As a matter of fact it was the hotel staff who should have been thanked.)

We were informed that the proceedings of the workshop would be sent to us later. I liked the idea. As I came out I weighed the load in my hands. It was around 3 kg. Together with the papers which were to follow, my collection would come in handy at the fag end of the month for the *raddi* hawker.

11

A VIP OCCASION

It was January 30, the day we pay homage to the Father of the Nation and those brave men who laid down their lives during the freedom struggle. (We are dutifully reminded of this fact every year by Akashvani and Doordarshan.)

I decided to visit Rajghat to pay my homage to Gandhiji and the other martyrs. The security men stopped me about three furlongs away from Bapu's Samadhi. They said they were not allowing anybody beyond a certain point.

A policeman said to me: "You can pay your homage after the leaders leave the place".

"But I want to be there at 11", I insisted.

"No, you can't," said the policeman point blank and pushed me further back from where I stood.

The VIPs—the President, the Vice-President, the Prime Minister and other Privileged persons—came one after the other.

There were no crowds around Rajghat. The D.T.C. drivers and the passengers inside their buses, motorists and those in three-wheelers and scooterists waited impatiently for the whole thing to be over so that they could move on to wherever they were headed for.

The sirens were sounded at 11 a.m. I stood at attention to observe the two minutes' silence. But I was making a fool of myself.

Everybody was moving around. Even the policeman before me puffed at his bidi. The driver of a Municipal Corporation truck carrying flower pots (intended for decorating the roadside) honked the horn to clear the traffic before him. Near the Delhi Gate crossing the traffic moved as usual.

At two minutes past 11 the sirens were sounded again. Those in the traffic jam heaved a sigh of relief and waited for the VIPs to go.

It was now all clear for me to go into Rajghat. The jawans with their rifles were rushing to board the trucks which were to carry them away. A few volunteers were still singing *Ram Dhun* for the benefit of a movie cameraman. Not more than 100 persons remained inside. Most of them were tourists both Indians and foreigners.

As I came out, I wondered if the Mahatma belonged only to VIPs.

12

COMPUTERISED BAPTISM

The day is not far off when parents will seek the help of computers before baptizing their offspring.

Except the orthodox; who may continue to open a holy book and take the first letter of the first word on the page before them as the first letter of the child's name, people are generally bound to turn to modern technology. But computers are not infallible and one may expect to see on their print-outs some very odd and funny names like "Colon", "Memory" and "Release".

It seems that in those parts of the world where computers have become an inseparable part of life couples are already making use of the "machines" to name their children. The little ones are duly christened "Sleep" "Smart", "Whatmore", etc.

The advent of computers notwithstanding change has been the essence of human life. Not so long ago names decided by the elders used to be accepted without a whimper. When children were named "Nandlal", "Vilayati Ram", "Natha Singh", "Mengha Singh", "Sharbati Devi", "Kotri Devi", "Munni Begum", "Wazir Kaur", "Angoori" or "Jaddan Bai", nobody had the guts to question the wisdom of those who had thought of these names.

Not that all the names were odd. "Bharat Bhushan", "Jati Rattan", "Rajendra" and "Rushid" were common among men and "Swaran", "Krishna", "Mehtab" and "Simran" were often chosen for women.

From an individual's name one could guess whether the person concerned had an urban or a rural background. For instance, "Kitabi" was sure to be from a village and "Krishan" from a town.

Every region in India has its own tradition with regard to names.

Eastern India, especially the States of Assam and Bengal, opted for modern names about a century ago. If one can find an 80-year-old "Siddhartha", an eight-year-old child with that name is also there.

Similarly if there is a 60-year old "Renuka", there is also a six-year-old girl with that name.

In western India not much change is discernible. "Sudhakara", "Shankarrao", "Yashodhara" and "Nirmala" can be found among both the old and the young.

In south India almost everybody, whether counting days or playing in the courtyard, bears the name of some god or goddess. As the father's (in the case of a boy) or the husband's (in the case of a married girl) name is prefixed to the name of the person concerned, it looks as if the tradition is being maintained without any change. If there are "Sankaras", "Ramas", "Ganpathis", and "Vasudevas" among the males, there are "Lakshmis", "Savitris", "Sitas" and "Rukminis" among the females. The classic example is that of Sivaramakrishnan, the noted cricketer.

The latest trend manifests itself in the dropping of the middle name. These days youngsters prefer to have only the first name and the surname. This trend may suit the computers.

Lest some wild guesses should be made about what the initials of this writer stand for. I wish to add that I was named after the Nobel laureate from Bengal.

13

CROWNING GLORY

I do not know about others at least I cannot afford the luxury of an aerated water bottle these days.

Ever since the spurt in prices of all the brands, I had been cooling myself with the chilled soft drinks at somebody else's cost. Marriages, mundan ceremonies, birthday parties and visits to the friends who are known for their hospitality, come in very handy. Personally I prefer a glass of cane-juice, especially the one named after a diminutive star of Hindi cinema.

But with every second company in the rat race of holding competitions of one type or the other, and offering fabulous prizes, there is always a temptation to go in for a drink, not to quench one's thirst but to try luck in grabbing a crown which may bring some prize or a trip abroad.

The craze for the crown collection compelled a host at a marriage reception recently to depute his son to be at the counter where the soft drinks were being served. The young boy did an excellent job. At the end of the reception he had collected around three hundred and odd crowns of a particular brand; many among them offering some prizes.

The elders may try to keep away from this crazy business of crown collection. But who can stop the kids.

"The plain, pure water only can quench one's thirst," I argue with them.

"Who said it is pure?" they shout back. "It is full of chlorine and mud."

Even if one speaks volumes about the qualities of cane-juice, the youngsters are not convinced. "The way it is prepared a glass of cane-juice should carry tons of dust particles," they counter.

The children laugh in their sleeves when they are told that our ancestors always preferred health-giving drinks like nimboo-pani, lassi, sattu and sardai. "They had no choice," we are told.

It seems there is no choice but to fall in line with others and be in the race of crown-count.

14

ON MOTHER INDIA

Yeh Desh we were told in kindergarten and primary classes, was once a *Sone Ki Chidiya*. The English rulers, who kept us slaves for more than two centuries, indulged in all sorts of *Loot Maar* and made the country poor.

But for the *Qurbani* of our elders we would not have been *Azad*. Many preferred *Phansi* to free us from the *Zanjeer* of *Ghulami*.

However, even after six decades of independence, we are nowhere near 'Gandhi's' dream of *Ram Rajya*. Even Nehru's desire to make India a *Sangam* of *Purab Aur Paschim* remains unfulfilled.

All these years there have been *Khoon Kharaba*. Sometimes *Bhai Bhai* have become *Jani Dushman* of each other. Gone are the days when a *Padosi* was ready to shed *Khoon Pasina* for the neighbour. Very often we have seen *Insaan* turning *Janwar*. *Pyar Mohabbat* is there only in name.

The protectors of *Kanoon* are helpful to the *Mujrim* and harass the *Masoom*.

Politicians of the day, whether *Aaj ka Ram Avtar* or 'Mr. Sampath', are concerned only with amassing *Dhan Daulat*. Only a 'Leader' who is *Chalak* in making all sorts of *Kasme Wade* and expert in *Hera Pheri* is *Kamyab*.

Corruption has become a part of our *Zindagi*. Nothing moves here without *Paisa*.

Mazdoor, whether in the village or in town, and *Shahari Babu* are still doing *Sunghursh* to survive. Their basic problem of *Roti*

Kapda Aur Makaan is very much there. Many die for want of *Roti* and *Ghar*. Many are still rotting their lives in *Badnam Bastis* and at the 'Railway Platforms'.

It is shameful that the *Dharti* that proudly talks of *Sati Savitri* and *Bahu Begum* has no respect for women. Many *Dulhans* are still being burnt alive for bringing insufficient dowries. Even the talk of women's *Izaat* sounds phoney when one reads the news of 'Rape'.

The young, whether 'Bobby' or 'Anita', 'Don' or *Rampur Ka Lakshman*, are not prepared to accept *Nasihat* which their elders administer to them *Raat Aur Din*. The talk of *Kranti* has not been able to inspire them. To them it is a word meant for *Kitaab* only. However, they are *Betaab* to see an *Inquilaab* in the country.

The talk of computers and the twentyfirst century are *Kora Kagaz* for all those who are living from hand to mouth.

But everything is not lost as yet. With the political and movie 'stars' having come out to serve 'Mother India', there is an *Aasha*. Soon we may be taking *Naya Kadam* towards a better India.

15

ALL FOR THE GUESTS

The other day somebody was talking about the asset preferences of the middle and lower middle classes in India and listed many items. However, I am inclined to include the people from the upper middle and high income groups also. The preferences of Indians, whether from south or north; east or west; rich or poor; are almost similar. The example is that of gold and jewellery. There must not be an Indian, who does not hanker after this metal.

But the gentleman, while referring to the assets, was not talking about gold and its by-products, which Indians prefer to keep in the bank lockers, but to the ones that are acquired as a matter of routine. The gentleman's talk forced me to look around my house and get an assessment done of the assets. To my surprise I found that 80 per cent of the assets in the house are earmarked for the guests only, which in Punjabi parlance means *ayae-gaye vaste.*

We have some crockery and cutlery (some imported too) which are taken out when some important guest, relation (my wife does not discriminate between her own and mine) or friend pays a visit to us. For our daily use we continue to have tea in glass tumblers and meals in the crockery purchased locally. Even the replenishments come only from *Shani Bazar*, that comes up every Saturday in our locality.

The cup-saucers and soup-bowls of bone-China and golden flowery dinner set are put to full use when a VIP is visiting us. But the tension (lest a piece is broken) that prevails during their use is probably more taxing than the pleasure of winning a kudo or two from the guests.

Then we have some linen—quilts, bed covers, cushions, pillow covers, etc.—which remains buried in the boxes of the Diwans till a worthy of its use visits us. On our part, we continue to use the inexpensive things, replacements (again from the local market) coming only when they have outlived their utility. Talking of linen, I am reminded of my mother who always kept aside some of the best linen for use of her *Damads* (my sisters' husbands).

The upkeep of the house also depends on the exposure of a particular portion to the outsiders. The concentration is on the drawing room or *Baithak* (the concept of living room is yet to catch up with the middle and lower income groups). It is always kept in spick-and-span condition; the lady of the house constantly reminding me and the children about its tidiness. After all we have to put our best foot forward for our guests.

We make it a point to keep away from our guests' eyes the junk of the house. It is stored in the lofts and boxes. However, it comes in very handy in getting stainless steel utensils, plastic-ware, garlic, etc.

All that I have detailed above do not suggest that anything unusual is happening in our house. What is true with us should hold good for many households. Probably the tradition of extending the best hospitality to the guests weighs with us. We do not want the guests to carry the impressions that they are not welcome.

16

WORKING LUNCH

"Let us move into the lunch room", announced the Director who was presiding over the group consisting of a dozen participants in a discussion on "New Techniques for Book-selling". "Let the lunch be a working one."

"A working lunch?", I almost whispered in concealed surprise to the participant sitting next to me. Seeing me in a perplexed frame of mind, he said: "The working lunch is now one of the most important features of the management technique. You discuss things while you are eating".

"But all through we have been told to do one thing at a time. How can you eat and discuss various matters together?"

He only smiled as we moved into the lunch room. The palatable and spiced menus provide good food for thought, I imagined.

For a change, the lunch was a sitting one. "A working lunch is like that only", I was told by another participant.

This being my first experience, I waited anxiously for the working lunch to start.

"There is not much of cucumber in the salad", shouted a woman participant. "It is all onions and tomatoes".

"These days cucumber is selling at Rs. 60 per kilogram. Probably you do not go to the market to buy vegetables", said a hefty participant with a bad throat.

(I had found him gulping down at least four bottles of coke and two cups of coffee with half-a-dozen biscuits during the coffee break.)

"And I am sure you are not aware of the new trends in book-selling", intervened the Director. He had almost repeated himself in the pre-lunch discussions also he had said the same thing.

"These days nobody treats a good book as a hot cake", somebody chipped in.

"Like cakes the books are also for the rich only", said the smart woman who had talked about the missing cucumber.

"Jokes apart", said the Director "we have to make the people aware that books are their best friends". He had again repeated himself.

"By telling the people so, we will make them believe that human beings are their enemies", said the gentleman with a bone in his mouth.

"Don't you feel that this precisely is happening in our country at the moment? People are fighting with one another over property, money and other materialistic things", philosophised the Director.

"The curd in the 'raita' is somewhat sour", said the hefty gentleman. Probably it was not going down his bad throat easily.

There was a spell of silence. One could only hear occasional orders for replenishments. However, some talked among themselves about power cuts, D.T.C. fares, video-piracy, etc.

"The subject requires a deep study", said the Director as the dessert was being served. There were sounds similar to those of the jaltarang as spoons played against ice-cream cups.

It was all over. A participant said to the Director: "Sir, the discussions were very thought-provoking". Probably he had done full justice to the lunch.

I could only smile at the statement and moved to the room where we were yet to thrash out the main subject.

17

WE TOO ARE CHAMPS

When the Prime Minister chided young men and praised girls (rather a girl) for their performance at the Asian Games, none might have taken him seriously. Many would have considered his remarks as another (prime) ministerial sermon or one of those pep talks which our politicians give day in and day out.

However, the under-performance at the games can be traced to many reasons; one being the non-inclusion of the games in which nobody can beat us.

Had there been a contest to pick up the best person in the game of gossiping, our participants would have won all the medals. There was no need to hold training camps or engage coaches. Just a round of the Government offices could have helped one in selecting the best team. Incidentally, this is one discipline in which we can offer to coach the participants of many others countries.

It is a tragedy that there was no competition for *bhashanbazi* (delivering speeches), the game in which we can beat anybody in the world, leave alone Asia. Here again, the selection of the participants would have been very easy. Our best could have been selected from among the Ministers, both at the Union and the State levels, and politicians of any hue. Our participants in this game were capable of creating records never to be shattered by anybody in future.

Makhanbazi (flattery) and *Chamchagiri* (sycophancy) are two other sports in which no country can take us on. The participants for these disciplines could be scouted from all walks of life without much difficulty.

Slogan-shouting is another field we specialize in. Whether it is shouting "long live" (*jindabad*) or "down down" (*murdabad*), no country in the world can match us. The picking-up of our representatives for this game too would not have presented any problem. There are specialists who can shout slogans for hours together without making their throats sore. Their voices are well-trained to shout any kind of slogan.

Holding demonstrations of any type and at any hour (temperatures—low or high—do not dampen the spirits of the demonstrators) is another event in which no country would be able to stand against us. There are persons who would be too willing to represent India at their own expense.

And, finally fasts-unto-death and relay fasts are disciplines in which nobody on this earth can beat us. There are experts (political veterans and trade union leaders) who can go without food for days without losing an ounce of weight. We can achieve knock-out victories in this game.

But my only worry is that in course of time other countries may also learn the tricks of these games and put us out of medal-reckoning.

18

THE REBAPTISING FEVER

When I referred to Mumbai as Bombay, a friend from the metropolis immediately corrected me. "Bombay is no longer spelt like that. It is now Mumbai," he said putting all emphasis on "M". And to bring home his point further, he said, "I wish you keep yourself abreast of the changes that have come about in the names of many cities and towns in the country."

Lest I am caught napping again, I decided to update myself with the changes. And to my surprise, I found that many towns and cities have been rebaptised, either by way of spellings or in name altogether. One may call the exercise a silent revolution.

Poona is now Pune. Vadodara is the new name for Baroda and Panjim is now known as Panaji. The simple Ooty has been given the tongue-twisting name of Udagamandalam. Jullundur is now spelt as Jallandhar.

Officially, Ropar in Punjab is now Roopnagar, Bhatinda is now Bathinda; the seat of Hindu religion, Banaras, is Varanasi; Simla is made Shimla; and Guhati is made Guwahati.

And if Gen. Sinha, who now lives in Patna has his way, shortly the state capital will be known as Patiliputra. And there must be many in India like Gen. Sinha and Bal Thackeray who would be working overtime, pouring over history book, to bring about changes in the names of cities and towns which, they think, need 'local' names.

Talking of this rebaptising process, I am reminded of the day when the English Cawnpore was changed to Kanpur. For days people talked and discussed about the change without coming to any conclusion.

Why and who work on these changes is rather difficult to know. Maybe, someone will throw more light on this rebaptising affair. Or maybe, a student of phonetics will like to probe further.

19

RIGHT-ABOUT TURN

Not that I was late, probably others were on time. Very rarely people are punctual for marriages and mournings.

But it came as a big surprise to find the shamiana overflowing with mourners. I could only squeeze myself into the rear rows.

What the learned pandit was saying was hardly audible. Probably the discourse was meant only for the family members and the ones who occupied the front rows.

The people sitting somewhat away from the dais talked in whispers; not caring for the solemnity of the occasion. Two gentlemen sitting ahead of me, colleagues of the deceased, too talked in low tones, but loud enough to reach my ears, I needed no extra effort to catch their conversation.

First gentleman (bringing his head close to the second): "It will be very hard for his wife to manage the affairs now".

Second gentleman (in a somewhat harsh tone): "I don't think so. The bastard had earned enough while he was in the purchase department."

The first gentleman cautioned him against speaking loudly. But his friend was not bothered and continued in the same tone: "He had invested a lot in land. Apart from his house here he had two plots, one each in Gurgaon and Chandigarh."

It seemed the first gentleman did not know much about the deceased. He said in a voice of disbelief: "I don't think your information is correct. Only a month back he had asked me for a loan."

The second gentleman had a mischievous smile on his face. "That used to be his habit," he said. "He took loans from all and sundry just to prove that he was a very honest man."

"But he told me that he needed money for his wife's medical check-up", the first gentleman clarified.

"All rubbish", said the second gentleman. "In fact he never cared for his wife. He was given to women and wine. His wife had even complained to the office to that effect." All these revelations shocked the first gentleman.

Meanwhile the pandit had finished and asked others to say a few words by way of homage to the deceased.

The first to get up was the gentleman who claimed to know the deceased well.

He spoke to the assembly on his own behalf and that of his other colleagues. He spoke of the honesty, dedication and straightforwardness of the dead man. He made a special mention about the concern he always had for his wife and children.

The first gentleman listened to his colleague with wide open eyes and a gaping mouth. I watched the scene with some amusement.

The moment the gentleman came back the first gentleman showered the former with all sorts of queries about what he had said about the deceased.

But the other coolly replied: "Do you think anybody would have believed me if I had told the truth."

The first gentleman could only nod in agreement.

20

A MATTER OF HEART

When, after looking at the ECG, the doctor informed me that there were some traces of strain on the heart, I was glad to note that at least I am not a heartless person.

I have been very often accused of being a man with no heart. The reason advanced is that I do not weep at the time of cremations and at the time of bidding farewell to the brides.

I wonder how shedding of tears on such occasions is related to the heart. Probably the tears of blood (can they be seen?) can reflect one's heart condition.

But heart does play a significant role in more than one way in one's life.

No romance can succeed unless the lovers are really united at heart. Failure in romance breaks the heart (one may not observe it or feel it) of many a lover.

There are many who take silly things to heart and mar their lives. However, they should know that by pouring out one's heart one can unburden oneself to a great extent.

The chicken-hearted or people with weak hearts are the ones who run away from the problem. They have no heart to fight the things out.

The heart-burns, whether contracted by overeating or by feeling jealous of others, are bad. The former may be cured by an antacid tablet or *churun*, but the latter can cause harm to one's health.

In medical parlance, to have an enlarged heart is no doubt something dangerous. But by being large-hearted one can earn good wishes and blessings of all and sundry.

Heart has been exploited to the hilt by men of letters, both of prose and poetry, especially of Urdu. If Ghalib could lament *Dil hi to hae na sangokhist*, Zafar's *Lagta nahin hae dil mera ujade deyar main* was heart-rending.

Hindi cinema too has given much importance to heart both by way of titling the movies *Dillagi, Dil Ek Mandir, Dil Hi To Hae, Dil Tera Diwana, Dil Deke Dekho, Do Dillon Ki Dastan*, etc. with all the emphasis on dil, and through dialogues and songs.

In these days of open-heart surgery and heart transplants, nobody should lose heart. The physicians and surgeons hold promise even for those who hum K.L. Sehgal's *Ab ji ke kya karenge jab dil he toot gaya.*

21

OUR MILKY WAY

It was my first day. Like a youngster going to college for the first time or a man reporting for duty in a new office, I was nervous.

All these years a home-delivery man had been providing our quota of milk at our doorstep. The need to go to a Mother Dairy booth had never arisen. But the sudden disappearance of the milkman found me standing at the tail end of a queue of more than one hundred people; most of them in their night attires, looking sleepy and anxious at the same time.

The cans they carried reflected their status. The ones who had shining stainless steel containers were certainly from the middle and upper middle income groups. There were others with zinc, plastic and other assorted types, obviously from a lower income strata. The poorer sections of the society probably never visit these booths. The small quantity of milk they need is bought from the neighbourhood *halwai.*

I had not imagined that there would be a crowd at the booth. I remembered how our hosts in Washington used to get their supplies from the department store in a matter of minutes. But then I remembered I was in India and any place without crowds and queues would be most abnormal.

A push from behind brought my train of thought to a halt. The queue had stretched further. Some fifty persons were now standing behind me. Some got restless because the queue did not move. Some grumbled against the man who distributed tokens. He was slow, no doubt. Some shouted at those who tried either to smuggle themselves into the queue or to get their supply by proxy. Some persons wanted the complainers to ignore all this, but they were promptly shouted down.

As the queue moved, at snail's pace of course, some sort of calm returned. At last there was only one man before me. I could see two green spots on the milk machine. I likened the machine to India. The people were milking it according to their capacity. The ones with 'money power' bought many tokens (probably for their pets also). But the majority confined themselves to two or three half-litre tokens. No economist was needed to figure out the 'haves' and the 'have-nots'.

As I approached the counter, the man behind the caged-window gave me a piercing look. Probably he could make out that I was a "fresher".

"Four tokens, please," I said handing over a tenner to him.

"You will get only two. Don't you see the long queue"?, he admonished me. I was shocked. The man who preceded me had purchased five tokens. "But"...

"No but-shut," the fellow said firmly. I wanted to dispute his discretionary power but was pushed aside by the people behind me.

As I moved to the queue of token-holders, I thought of Dr. Kurien's oft-repeated slogan of "Operation Flood". We don't need a flood—just a good trickle down the milk machine, I mused to myself.

22

THE SOLO SHOW

I am not a lover of art and the things connected with it. But when a painter-friend approached me for some financial help to enable him to hold an exhibition of his paintings, I just could not say no.

I knew he was very sincere and hard working and very badly needed a boost. He was sure that by holding "a show" of his "works" he would be able to get the recognition without which no painter could sustain himself for long.

A gallery was hired for three days at a centrally located place. The gentlemen of the Press, especially those who matter in the field of art, were specially requested both through written communication and on phone to cover it.

The hectic search for a VIP to inaugurate the exhibition, however, proved futile. Whoever my friend approached asked some odd questions: "Have you held an exhibition earlier? What will the gathering be like? Have you made arrangements for the coverage on television?" etc. In desperation my friend finally had to request his Director (a man with no aesthetic sense to have appreciated his paintings) to be the Chief Guest. He also asked one of his colleagues to take pictures on the occasion.

The D-day came. Since the painter had made transport arrangements, there was a fair collection of his colleagues to welcome the CG and grace the occasion. None came from the Press and naturally there was no mention of the show in the papers next day. The CG kept us waiting and also in suspense for about one hour. Finally he came but was disappointed to see only familiar faces.

As the CG cut the ribbon, he was garlanded by my friend's wife. The camera clicked to take the snaps. He took exactly six minutes to take a round of the gallery and to have a look at about 40 paintings. He evinced no special interest in any of the creations of the painter.

Coffee and snacks were served and then everybody dispersed. My friend dutifully kept the visitor's book at the exit for the patrons to give their valued comments.

All the three days I made it a point to visit the gallery where my friend waited in vain for the visitors. My presence did cheer him up. But of patronage, there was no sign.

A couple along with their two kids did come but only to take shelter from the sharp showers that had lashed one of the evenings.

Dejected by the poor response my friend wound up the show three hours before the scheduled time. He took a vow not only to have no further exhibitions of his works, but never to touch the painter's brush again. I felt sorry for him but did not know how to bring him back on the track.

I had forgotten the wasted essay till I read a news-item that the CG, who had reluctantly agreed to inaugurate my friend's exhibition, had been elected president of a very prominent cultural group of the city and was tipped to lead a delegation going abroad. I was somewhat shocked and immediately contacted my friend to confirm.

"Yes, it is true," he said and added, "the snap my colleague took at the time of my show has done the trick. An enlarged picture of the occasion not only adores his room in the office but also his drawing room for everybody to see and for him to claim that he is a great lover of art."

23

GOOD MORNING, CITY FOLKS

Cocks no more herald the dawn now. At least I am not aware of it. Or may be they are still on their jobs in the rural areas.

The urbanites, however, with many other gadgets to help them, do not depend any more on the cocks. Apart from the time-tested alarm clocks, there are now wrist-watches which chime the alarms at the fixed hours, and the telephone (in case you have one) operators to wake you up with their sweet "Good Mornings".

The elderly persons (with age they become poor sleepers) are probably the best to rely upon. They will dutifully wake the other inmates of the house, primarily to release the tensions build-up during the sleepless nights. My grandfather used to wake the grandmother up before going for his morning walk by striking her cot with his walking stick. I am also maintaining the tradition but in different way. I wake my wife up by offering her a cup of tea.

Unlike villages where the morning starts on a sober and peaceful note, the dawn in cities is heralded with all sorts of noises. The frequent pulling of the chains of the W.C.; sweeping of the floors by pulling and pushing the household fixtures; rinsing of the laundry in the washing machines; persistent pressing of the call bells by the maidservants; switching on the radios and transistors; horn-honks of the milkmen; calls of the street vendors, etc., have all become parts of the morning life in the cities.

A *raddiwala* is always the first to visit our block followed by a bread vendor.

"Why do you come so early? I don't think you get any business at this hour," I once asked the *raddiwala*. With a mischievous smile he replied, "The babus are always hard pressed for the money and I help them in my own way. I have a permanent clientele and they always welcome me, especially during the last days of the month."

The bread vendor is popular because he gives things on credit—a boon for the babus.

Mornings can be different for different people. There are individuals, irrespective of the fact whether they are residing in remote villages or metropolitan cities, who are very superstitious about their dawns. A relation of mine prefers to look at his palms before facing others. Similarly, a friend will not talk unless he has said his prayers. Yet there is another gentleman who first looks at himself in the mirror before looking at others.

A resident of our block avoids his immediate neighbour in the morning because he considers him unlucky. At the same time there is a gentleman who takes a circuitous route to wish good morning to another resident whom he thinks is very lucky for him.

But my hats off to an aged resident of our block who invariably wishes good morning to all those he comes across and gives neem-twigs for brushing the teeth if one desires to have one. Isn't it the best way to say a very good morning?

24

FROM "TAMAS" TO TWILIGHT

It was surprising that some people should have made such a big hullabaloo against the TV serial "Tamas". There was nothing in it to get worked up. Nobody can deny that we had had (and continue to have) worst communal riots in free and secular India and I do not think that these riots have changed adversely the outlook of the people at large. The two incidents that took place at that time would prove my contention.

My father who worked for a newspaper in Lahore refused to migrate to India despite the pleadings of my mother and other relations. He was of the firm view that there would never be a mass exodus, and definitely not on a communal basis. He thought it to be a temporary "madness". He wanted his proprietors to start a Pakistan edition of the paper from Lahore.

Since he was adamant, my mother was left with no option but to stay back with him even after Pakistan had come into existence. And then one day a dozen Pathans raided our house, looted it, and shot dead my father but spared my mother. She had to leave the place and come to India.

I had imagined that she would be bitter and pour venom against those who murdered her husband. But when I met her she was cool, calm and composed. She did not utter a single word that would have vitiated my mind. She merely narrated the gory incident and finally said: "We have made our contribution to the freedom struggle. Instead of a Britisher shooting him down somebody else did it." That was the statement that helped my young mind to grow without bitterness or bigotry.

The second incident which I have not been able to forget till date, took place a couple of months before the subcontinent was divided, although the communal tensions had already reached a point where it needed only a spark to start a conflagration.

A boy named Dost Mohammed, whose father, a Fire Officer, had lost his life saving a Hindu family, sought admission in our school run by a "Sabha". He was admitted to our section. In a class of about 70 he was the lone Muslim (or perhaps in the school). All of us, including the teacher, were surprised because the Islamia School was only a few yards from our school.

No one in the class was ready to befriend Dost Mohammed. I went out of my way to be friendly with him. But that invited boos and jeers for both of us from other classmates. This created a problem for the teachers.

One day our class teacher asked his mother to come to the school. I accompanied Dost Mohammed to the staff room where his mother had come to see the teacher.

"Why do you want your son to study in this school? Couldn't you manage his admission in 'your' school?" the class teacher asked.

She was prompt in her reply. "About Islam he can learn at home itself. It is to learn about your religion and culture that we sent him to 'your' school." The teacher was too dumbstruck to speak.

As she took leave of the class teacher, she said: "If it is really a problem for you to have Dost in your school, he will not come from tomorrow." That was the last we saw of Dost. But to this day I cherish the nobility of my friend's mother.

25

FESTIVAL SIDELIGHT

The traffic came to a screeching halt when the policeman waved it to stop. A VIP was on his way to inaugurate the Russian circus, a part of the festivities connected with the USSR festival in India.

A boy aged around ten, who was busy helping his mother at a building site, came running to the pavement. The curiosity to see the motorcade that was to come had probably brought him over to the place where he stood.

His mother shouted, "Hey, Ramiya come back and help me." He ignored his mother's call and continued to stand there. By now a good number of people had come over to the pavement, impatiently waiting to cross over to the other side.

His mother had stopped working and anxiously waited for her son to come back and join her. A supervisor, who was overseeing the work-force shouted at her: "Why have you stopped your work? Let the chap go to hell." Reluctantly she continued with the work.

The boy had become a part of the crowd that now stood at the pavement. He separated himself from it and came close to the policeman. "Who is coming? Is there some 'tamasha'?" he asked the policeman pointing towards the venue of the circus.

Not in a mood for any conversation, the policeman gave him a nasty look and pushed him back to the pavement. I doubted whether the policeman knew at all who was coming and what for.

The boy was getting restless. He craned his neck out only to be pushed back again by the gentleman who had lost his balance because of the manner the boy had elbowed him. "Will there be some 'khel' Babuji?" he asked the gentleman. "Even if it is there, it should not concern you," the Babuji admonished him.

The boy's mother, who had lost sight of the boy, walked to the pavement and caught hold of him by his neck. "You idiot can't you look after your sister? She is crying" she chided him.

The boy wriggled himself of his mother's grip and ran back to the pavement. The hapless mother started breast-feeding the crying child. The supervisor looked furiously at her; his eyes getting jammed at her bare breast. His lips quievered to say something but he suppressed it.

A police jeep with its siren blaring zoomed past the point where the boy stood. Pushing and jostling he surged ahead to have a glimpse of the motorcade. In the process he slipped and fell on the road. The policeman charged him with his baton, striking him twice or thrice.

It hardly took two minutes for the motorcade to pass. The road which looked deserted a few minutes back was teeming with traffic again.

The crowd on the pavement had dispersed. Lost in his thoughts (or fantasies), the boy stood alone there. To him the festival meant nothing.

I was sure he would not be able to cross over to the other side of the road to see the circus.

26

KAMAACHI

We were really taken by surprise when one morning Kamaachi, the part time domestic help, brought two cans full of ready-to-fry mixture for "dosas" and "vadas". About 30 to 40 "vadas" and as many "dosas" could be made from the stuff she had brought.

"Make 'dosas' and 'vadas' for your son-in-law and daughter," she told my wife. "Let it be a treat from my side." We were touched by her gesture.

Kamaachi felt offended when I suggested to my wife that she be duly compensated for the stuff. I was sure that she had spent about Rs. 50. "Can't I give a treat to your daughter and son-in-law?" she queried, and added. "After all, I have always treated your daughter like my own." Her eyes had moistened as she spoke. I regretted injuring her feelings.

Then, in a tone that was both bitter and pathetic she said: "I wish I could also serve my son-in-law in the manner you do."

We know that her only daughter, Rani, whom she had married off about three years ago and who is pregnant for the second time, is not being treated properly by her husband, a fact Kamaachi very often tells my wife and seeks her advice on the problem.

Rani's husband has proved to be a good-for-nothing fellow. He does nothing and wants his wife to feed him and the family, which includes his mother and unmarried sister. In addition to that, he expects Rani to ensure his usual quota of hooch and money for gambling. If she fails to do so, she is only given beatings not only by her husband but also his mother and sister.

And poor Kamaachi, in her anxiety to "settle" and ensure "happiness" for her daughter, works overtime to earn not only to support her own family of four but also that of her daughter.

"Why don't you ask your husband to talk to Rani's husband and tell him to mend his ways?" my wife asked Kamaachi one day.

"Rani's father cares two hoots for what happens to his daughter," Kamaachi replied with sarcasm. "In fact, he has been behaving with me in a similar beastly manner all these years. I am sure Rani will also get used to all this." It seems both Kamaachi and her daughter have resigned themselves to their fates.

The latest news, however, is very disturbing. Rani's husband has threatened to marry another woman and will relent only if Rs. 5,000 is given to him. Probably it will take years for Kamaachi and Rani together to earn this amount. Will he wait? Probably not.

Sometimes I wonder whether Kamaachis and Ranis do not outnumber Kiran Bedis in this land of Sitas and Savitris.

27

DROUGHT DINNER

There could not have been a better place than the banquet hall of a five-star hotel to hold dinner for the participants of a seminar on droughts. After all, they had put their heads together to thrash out a dry and drab issue like the drought.

That the participants were dying of hunger was evident from the manner they had rushed to the dining hall the moment the chair declared the discussion closed and invited everybody to join for dinner. As a matter of fact the majority had stayed "put" and suffered the discussions only in anticipation of dinner.

The scene at the dining table was seen to be believed. The participants fell on each other to grab plates and pour themselves platefuls of the dishes laid out. Those who waited for their turn looked worried as they were not too sure whether anything would be left for them.

A participant was telling another colleague: "I don't think there will be any drought this year. That Baba at Mathura is sure to succeed in his mission and there will be plentiful rains." The other gentleman noded and said, "The organizers should have invited him and heard his views". A third gentleman intervened: "I am going to suggest to the government to have a separate laboratory for Yagnas." The three-some had a hearty laugh.

Some of the participants tried to catch the attention of the VIP, who had delivered the inaugural address. He had thrown a hint that the organizers were thinking of sending a delegation to Ethiopia to study the conditions prevailing in that country at the time of the drought. There was a mad race to curry favour with him. He was being praised for his "excellent and thought-provoking" speech, though everybody knew it was banal.

One of the organizers was asking a participant: "Have you visited the States which are worst-affected by the drought?"

"Not exactly. But I have read about the conditions in the drought-hit areas," came the reply.

As the VIP finished his meals, a stream of people ran to get ice-cream for him. "Ice-cream is his weakness," somebody had said.

A participant shouted at the bearer for giving him a burnt chappati. The bearer apologized and rushed to get the replacement. "The drought-hit people do not get even burnt chappatis," somebody remarked.

There was a sudden commotion in a corner. One of the lady participants had pointed out that a particular gentleman was a "fake" one, and was only substituting his boss. The organizers retrieved the situation by pointing out that he was supposed to prepare notes for his boss and submit a report. Later it transpired that the lady herself was accompanying her boss and had come to the seminar to provide company to him.

No sooner had the VIP left the hall, the other participants made a beeline towards the exit, though the organizers had requested them to stay on to exchange notes on the discussions held so far. But probably for them it was all over with the dinner.

Somebody, who was very active at the time of question-answer session, was telling another participant: "This is probably the last seminar on drought. We are expecting a very good monsoon this year."

"But then we can hold a seminar on floods," said the other participant.

"And dinner too," said the first gentleman hopefully.

28

SPECIALISTS' DENS

Look around your locality, or, for that matter your block, and you are sure to come across a poly-clinic, if not more. Go near it and you will find a big board staring at you listing the "specialists" whose services are available to cure you of your illnesses.

There are "cardiologists", "radiologists", "gynaecologists", "ophthalmologists", etc. with the sole aim of providing "relief" to the "sick" and "suffering", of course, for money only.

Physicians and surgeons wholly depend on these places for getting the diagnosis done and "pin-pointing" the disease. The doctors have only to prescribe a medicine. As a matter of fact, these "diagnostic centres" and doctors have become complementary to one another and have made the latter's job "easy".

A medical practitioner these days is not considered "learned" unless he does not asks patients to undergo some "tests". Even if you are having a "common cold" or an "irritating throat", the doctor is certain to prescribe some "pathological tests", though ultimately he may tell you that "nothing is wrong with you" and what you need is "a protein-rich diet" and a "brisk walk in the morning".

The immediate feeling one gets on entering any of these "poly-clinics" is that of a lobby of a five-star hotel. There is a lady receptionist to welcome you and cheer you up. A smiling lady is bound to give a boost to your sagging spirits. There are "sofas" and "settees" to make you comfortable and in case you want you can be served with hot and cold drinks at the rates that will beat any top class restaurant.

I sometimes wonder how in an age when the "specialists" are ruling the roost, the "vaids" and "hakims" still continue to "diagnose" the disease just "by feeling the pulse of the patient" and they rarely go wrong.

Similarly, Homoeopaths still treat their patients on the basis of the histories and symptoms. And there are vaids, hakims and Homoeopaths in their respective disciplines.

And finally some advice to the proprietors of these specialists' dens. They must recruit some "astrologists" to study the horoscopes of the patients and advise them as to how to ward off their *sad-sattis* and "bad periods" and which "doctor" or "specialist" to rely upon.

After all we Indians are a superstitious lot.

29

A FAST UNTO DEATH

I do not know who advised him, but his willingness to undertake a fast unto-death, as he himself put it, "to espouse the cause of his comrades in the office," really surprised many. The one who would not even miss a meal was being asked to fast for God knows how many days.

I had never seen him actively participating in trade-union activities. He was only known for his "participation in slogan-shouting demonstrations".

His worried wife came to me to ask me to stop him from undergoing this ordeal. "He is serious about it," she told me, "and may die". I wanted to tell her that so far as my knowledge went only one person had died by the sort of fast her husband was to undertake. But he looked determined and refused to listen to his wife's appeals.

Within hours of his agreeing, a shamiana was fixed outside the premises of his office and durries spread. It being winter, he was provided with a bedding, a blanket and a quilt.

He was garlanded and brought to the venue by his slogan shouting colleagues. He made a fiery speech listing the demands and finally declared that unless the management agreed to them, he would not break his fast. There were claps and slogans of "zindabad" for him. As dusk fell, everybody departed leaving the place to him, a colleague and a one policeman.

The second day started with a speech of a trade union activist who lauded him for his fast. His colleagues in groups gave him company but, later on, busied themselves playing games of

"Rummy" and "Sweep". The day ended with the speech of another leader.

The third day saw arrival of press reporters and photographers. He was interviewed and his snaps taken. During the day, a senior manager of his office wanted to see him. But his "colleagues" shouted slogans against him and compelled him to retreat.

The fourth day, a team of doctors came to examine him. They jotted down something on a piece of paper and handed it over to the sub-inspector of police on duty. A rumour spread that he was sinking. His wife with his two kids rushed to the site and pleaded with him to break his fast. He only looked helplessly at her.

On the fifth day, the management invited a delegation of "striking employees" for talks. While the members of the negotiation team enjoyed tea and snacks inside an air-conditioned room, he was left outside to continue "eating dust".

The news came that "an agreement" had been reached and that the managing director would help him break his fast by offering him a glass of lemon juice. Thus ended his five-day old fast-unto-death. He was profusely garlanded and taken round the office complex in a procession.

I felt relieved on hearing that he had undergone the ordeal successfully, though I had never an iota of doubt that he would not see it through. At the first opportunity, I met him and congratulated him and then asked him a question that had been weighing on my mind while he was on fast.

"How did you sustain yourself without food all these days?"

He looked straight at me and gave a broad smile. "This is a secret," he replied. "I would not like to divulge and put into trouble all those who may like to undergo similar fasts in future."

He is now an "expert" in undertaking hunger-strikes.

30

A MATTER OF MOODS

Mood is probably that state of mind which is reflected in an individual's outward behavior. But at the same time it is very difficult to read a person's mood by just looking at him. As they say appearances can be deceptive.

A calm and composed looking person may turn out to be a volcano, if he or she is not in a mood to talk or listen. However, it is very annoying to find a person getting out of sort on every filmy grounds. Even a nice joke may make him flare up.

In the offices juniors closely observe the moods of their seniors before confronting them. An urgent file or a letter may wait Sahib's signatures till it is known that he is in good mood. I know of a personal secretary of a very senior government official who every morning telephones his boss's wife to get a brief on her husband's mood. There is every possibility that a small tiff or an unpleasant happening at home may have spoiled the Sahib's mood.

Many continue to be out of mood and will not start their daily routines in their offices till they have consumed their usual quota of tea and coffee.

Students in schools and colleges watch the moods of their teachers before getting up to ask questions or raise queries. Similarly teachers too usually gauge the moods of the students before starting their classes. In either case moods can spoil the class room atmosphere.

The moods govern our personal lives too. The husbands may watch the moods of the spouses before even having a puff. The wives observe the moods of the hubs before talking business, especially when it comes to buying a new saree or a piece of jewellery. They may serve them with their favourite dishes to cheer them up. But if not in mood even the best cooked food may not be appreciated by them. However, in case they are in a jovial mood; spicy food or a hot curry gets the demand cleared.

There are many who get into their moods only when they are showered with praise, though they may not be deserving it.

One can understand and appreciate the moods of the elders. But when the kids talk of moods it looks really amusing. Recently I heard a five-year old child telling his mother that he was in no mood to do the homework. The mother only looked helplessly at the little one.

However, one thing is certain about the moods. They can make or mar situations, days and even personal relations. But my only wish is that somebody should invent a thermometer or some other device to gauge a person's mood. Maybe, someone somewhere is working on it.

31

FAST DEVELOPMENT

Rome might not have been built in a day, but Lal Bahadur Shastri Nagar in our colony was built in less than 24 hours.

It was six in the morning. The day had just dawned and there was not much activity on the roads of the colony. All of a sudden a dozen trucks, loaded with men, women and children stopped near a plot earmarked for a primary school. All of them were waving the flags of a political party. In a matter of minutes they stormed the vacant plot.

They were led by a kurta-pyjama-clad gentleman (presumably a "leader" of the political party, whose flags fluttered atop the trucks). He almost led them by the nose. He gave them detailed instructions regarding the whole operation.

Two truck-loads of thatch, cane, bamboos, etc. arrived and the "leader" took charge of the work of their distribution. A make-shift tea stall served tea and snacks (free, I presume) to everybody. All of them had chapattis and dal around noon. By the evening more than 80 per cent of the job had been completed.

The operation continued during the night also. By the early hours of the following morning the shanties made their presence strongly felt on the fast-changing face of the colony.

The leader oversaw the operations all along and kept both the police and the local residents away.

For quite a long period almost everybody one or two families continued to build their huts. Soon it was a slum in full bloom having hand-pumps, temporary lamp-posts which drew power from the junction pole, khokhas selling articles of daily use and, of course, a temple to pray to God seeking His protection against eviction.

The party flag fluttered on the tops of the huts.

The "leader" was seen roaming practically daily in the basti and heard saying that he would undertake a fast unto death in case the authorities tried to remove the inhabitants.

After a few days I learnt that he was a prospective candidate for the Municipal Corporation election from the ward in which this basti fell.

32

SNAKES AND LADDERS

If you have not played snakes and ladders, or having played it are still a poor player, a visit to Udyog Bhavan in New Delhi (or, in fact, any other Government department) will give you enough experience to master the game.

A non-resident Indian friend, eager to come back and serve his motherland, had asked me to make enquiries from the "right people" regarding his proposal for setting up an industrial unit. Armed with a letter, which gave a complete blueprint of his project, I proceeded to Udyog Bhavan.

My first stop was the "Enquiry" counter. After answering a few relevant and a few irrelevant questions I was directed by the man at the counter (who seemed more interested in his tea and pakoras than visitors) to go to room number 425 on the fourth floor. He then handed over to me the necessary entry slip. I decided to climb the staircase instead of taking the only lift which was working at that hour. One of the other two lifts was being kept ready for a VIP who was expected shortly and the second one was under repair.

I located the room. There were half a dozen persons in the room. It was some time before I caught the eye of the gentleman who looked like the boss.

"Yes?" he enquired in a commanding tone.

I told him the purpose of my visit.

"Who directed you to come over here?" he asked.

"The man at the 'Enquiry'." I replied.

"That fellow is no good. Your subject is dealt with by...section". And he mentioned a code name which made no sense to me.

"On which floor is the section?" I asked.

"Third", he said and helpfully added: "Second room in the left wing."

I climbed down to the third floor and located the place which looked like a record room. Not a soul was present there.

I knocked at the door of the adjacent room. There was no response. But I opened the door only to find two ladies engaged in knitting. My entry made no difference to their concentration, and they continued with their job. One of them, however, took papers from me and gave them a quick glance.

"Go to the fourth floor, room number 417," she advised me.

I did. Room number 417 was occupied by a man who had joined the section on that very day.

"I have not been assigned any duties yet," he told me, but was kind enough to make further enquiries from the "Enquiry" counter and asked me to go to room number 210 on the second floor.

The gentleman in room number 210 was good enough to ask me to take a seat. He took the papers from me and started reading them. He muttered "good", "very good", and nodded his head, probably in appreciation of the project my friend had prepared. I thought that I had, after all, succeeded in my mission, but was told that I had come to the wrong section again.

"I am afraid you will have to go to 'Enquiry' again," he finally announced.

I collected the papers and dashed down the staircase. As I passed by the "Enquiry" counter I heard the clerk ordering more tea.

After all this I have decided to write to my friend that he can serve his motherland better by remitting foreign exchange.

33

DEMOTED DREAMS

I did not know who took the initiative, but the manner his colleagues came forward to lend "a helping hand" had really surprised me. In a matter of two hours a tidy sum of eight hundred rupees was collected for his cremation.

What surprised me most was that a person who was a nonentity a day earlier was given an "official funeral". Hearse and buses were arranged to take his body and his colleagues to the cremation ground. Wreaths were specially got made and placed on his body on behalf of the Chairman and the M.D. Probably the circumstances—he was crushed to death by a bus while he was crossing the road—in which he died, had created an empathy for the deceased and his family. A thought that he might have committed suicide by allowing the bus to run over him also lurked large in my mind. However, I wished the money collected and spent could have been given to his widow.

I regretted that a person who all through his fifteen years of service had been wronged, ignored and even shunned, was given a tearful (crocodile, I was sure) funeral. He was denied even what was due to him. He simply wanted to be promoted as "a clerk". The stigma of being only "a daftary" had always made him sad.

"My son and daughter feel small when they are told that they are the children of a daftary," he had once told me. He had talked of dreams of seeing his son becoming a big officer and occupying "a cabin" and his daughter getting an officer as husband. To maintain a respectable profile he had started using the chartered bus. It was only in the chartered bus I developed acquaintance with him.

On my request he had improved his qualification (he graduated through correspondence) and acquired proficiency in typing. I had also helped him in drafting many a representation for the kind consideration of the people who mattered in his office. But both the "luck" and "his seniors" never favoured him. Those who were one-up in keeping the seniors in good humour used to "carry the day". When once I had advised him to take his cue from all those who knew the art of "pleasing" the "bosses", he flatly refused by saying, "I would rather die than stoop so low."

Then he suddenly became indifferent to everything. He stopped talking about his promotion and dreams, probably, he had resigned himself to his fate and left everything to the destiny. One day be suddenly disappeared till I heard of his tragic end.

Probably I would not have known about his family but for an unexpected meeting with his son. It was one of those bandh days and the buses were off the road. I was looking for an auto-rickshaw or a shared cab when somebody called me, "Come on Uncle, I will take you to your office." I looked around and saw a young man in his early twenties beckoning me. As I occupied his vehicle he told me, "You do not know me but I know you." He then narrated how after his father's death he had to leave his studies and purchase the three-wheeler for a living (his father's office had only offered him a daftary's post). He had already married off his sister to a latheman in a factory. Both he and his mother who also did errands in the neighbourhood, were trying to clear the loans they had taken at the time of his sister's marriage.

As I paid him off (he refused initially to accept anything and unlike others of his tribe charged only as per the meter), I felt sorry for him, his mother and sister. But from his looks I could feel that unlike his late father he did not believe in day dreaming.

34

THE SMARTER GANG

I knew I was inviting trouble when I objected to the infiltration of some students into the queue at the bus stop. They came in ones and twos and pushed me back from number three to about fifteenth position.

"We do it everyday uncle, and nobody raises any objection," I was told almost in a chorus.

"That does not give you licence to do whatever you like," I retorted.

"We have the licence," said bespectacled youngster in a satirical tone. He took out his DTC student concessional pass to prove his point. There was a chorus of laughter.

"It seems he is not aware of it," commented a girl who stood a little away from me and provided another comic relief to her friends.

"Poor old owl," whispered yet another girl, though loud enough to reach my ears.

I was stung. "I don't think you talk like that to your parents, girl," I protested.

She looked at me, not knowing how to react. But some of her male friends did look menacingly at me.

As this wordy duel continued none from among those who stood in the queue came to my rescue, though they were equally affected by the infiltration. However, an elderly gentleman advised me, "Let them enjoy, they are all young."

"Should it be at the cost of discipline?" I asked.

"Don't talk of discipline. We know how disciplined the elders are," roared one of the youngster.

"But somewhere a beginning has to be made," I retaliated. "And as they say 'catch them young', it has to be with you people."

"Oh, I see," exclaimed the girl who had called me "an owl". "So, you are trying to act as a reformer. Give him a big hand guys." There was again a chorus of **ha ha** and **hi hi.** I had to retreat. Single handed it was not possible to take them on.

The bus came and the queue was nowhere to be seen. From somewhere came more of their tribe and joined them. Two of them marked me and blocked my way to ensure that I did not get a seat and they did succeed in their "mission".

As I stood with my onc hand on the holding-rod and the other carrying the brief case, they mocked at me.

As the bus reached the Gole Market stop, the driver brought to a halt to allow another group of students to come in from the front door. From the manner they exchanged pleasantries with the driver, it seemed they were "regulars" in the bus.

The face of one of them looked somewhat familiar (later it transpired that he resided in our block). He pushed his way and came to me. "Why don't you share a seat with somebody?" he asked.

"But that depends on somebody. Isn't it?"

"I will manage for you," and pointing towards the boy who had shown me the DTC pass, he said, "Hay, you get up and allow uncle to sit." (Incidentally he and his friends also managed seats for two old ladies and one with a babe in arms.) The boy who was acting like a hero at the bus stop coolly got up and offered his seat to me. I was surprised, rather shocked. There were no protests, not even murmurs from his "comrades".

I was eager to talk to the "boy" who had managed the seat for me. We got down at the same stop. I gave him the account of what had happened at the bus stop, and asked, "How come none protested when the boy vacated seat for me?"

He gave a mischievous smile and replied, "Don't think we are different from the lot that misbehaved with you. We are no saints either. The targets—theirs and ours—are also the same. If they impress the girls by trying to show off, we do the same by exposing these paper heroes and in the process win your favour also." He laughed as he ended his explanation.

I was prepared to believe him. Only a few minutes back I was a witness to both the situations. But who ultimately succeeded in impressing the girls, I wasn't too sure.

35

MERA BHARAT MAHAAN

It was like any other Sunday with tensions started building up right from the word "go".

The nagging fear that the water supply, erratic as it had been for the past one month or so, might ditch any time, kept my wife and me on our toes for the best part of the morning. Even the morning cup of tea was taken under tension with water playing hide and seek.

The newspaper had nothing to cheer us up. The news of death and destruction, mostly man-made, dominated the front page. The forecast for the coming week that the "health of self and spouse may be adversely affected" and "suffering of a temporary setback to memory" further dampened the spirits.

I tried to locate a single bright spot in the newspaper. There was none. Whether it was politics, economy or sport, the scene presented a bleak outlook.

I switched on the television. The newscast sounded stale. The programme "slim and trim" could evoke no interest. We had already been through grueling exercises by way of lifting buckets of water to ensure supply for the day.

There was a sudden power shutdown. Probably somebody in Punjab or Haryana had decided to teach a lesson or two to Delhiites for "misusing" the "power". But I was sure that electricity would be back before the start of the teleserial 'Mahabharat". And it did.

The tap in the bathroom started trickling. I rushed to take a bath and thanked the Chief Minister of Haryana for extending the courtesy.

A friend telephoned to inform me that not only he had managed the "domicile" certificate but also the admission of his son in a State which had declared that "domicile" rule would be strictly adhered to.

Probably the money played the trick.

Again there was a power shutdown. To make my mind off from the afternoon heat I went through the matrimonial columns. Ninety per cent of the advertisers were seeking matches from their own castes, communities and regions. Similarly there were very few who wanted no dowry. Rather there were promises of 'decent' marriages.

The electricity was back. I switched on the television. A regional film with sub-titles in English was being telecast. It was a first rate movie. But I wondered how many would be following the English sub-titles.

A friend and his wife came to make a courtesy call. They had all the praise for the delicious dosas and sambhar they had at a South Indian wedding. "Why don't you get a Tamilian wife for your son?" I suggested. They ignored my suggestion. Probably they would like to have a daughter-in-law who could make good *alu-ka-paranthas*.

The Sunday evening feature film was a repeat telecast. But the commercials, especially on drinks and detergents provided some relief. However, I wished that somebody would venture on a drink and a detergent which could cool down our tempers and cleanse our souls.

The latest newscast added nothing to my information. The only news that interested us was regarding Delhi being put on red-alert; which meant more traffic jams and harassment.

As I got up to switch off the television I was reminded by Doordarshan that "My Bharat is Mahan". That gave me some hope and I felt somewhat reassured.

36

COURT ROOM SHOCK

Things turned out to be altogether different from what I had visualized before appearing as a prosecution witness in the court. Unlike the court-room scenes depicted in films and now on telescreens, there was utter chaos both inside and outside the Tis Hazari court rooms.

The case—theft of telephone instrument transformers in the office—in which I was to appear, was listed number two. The first case was Munni Devi versus the State.

The scene inside the court room could only be described as bedlam. The broken chairs and soiled benches provided in the room were already occupied. The lawyers and their clients were running in and out after whispering to the reader.

The clock hung above the magistrate's chair ticked away the minutes as we waited for the proceedings to start. In films clocks play a very important role. The presiding officers are always shown occupying their chairs sharp at ten and rising for the day when the clock strikes five. It was already eleven and the magistrate was nowhere in sight. The chaos continued.

Ultimately at about 11.30 the magistrate entered the court room. Barring the ones who were close to the dais or like me had no place to sit, none bothered to stand up. Again, unlike in the movies talking and jostling had continued unabated.

Munni Devi was called. She came in escorted by two lady-cops. She was accused of soliciting for prostitution. Standing as I was in the rear, I didn't know what transpired but the lady was whisked away after about ten minutes. Maybe I had seen too many movies, I expected a dramatic entry of her mother claiming that her daughter was innocent and the real culprit was only she (the mother) because she forced her to indulge in this immoral act. There would be whispering sounds in the court room compelling the magistrate to say "order order". But nothing of the sort happened.

Next my name was called. I rushed to the witness box and waited for the court clerk to bring Holy Gita and ask me to say on oath that I would tell the truth and nothing but the truth. But to my surprise the public prosecutor straightway started asking questions. I replied to all the questions as tutored.

I observed the magistrate. He was engrossed in some file. Probably for him it was a routine affair. There was no cross-examination by the defence counsel who only asked me to identify the accused; which I did. In fact I could not have forgotten him. The day he stole the transformers I had offered him tea and snacks.

I waited for somebody to enter the court room and announce that the innocent looking man who was being accused of theft, was only a victim of circumstances. The real culprits were those who asked him to do this dirty job to make good the shortages in the stores. But nothing dramatic or sensational took place.

"That is all," said the public prosecutor. "You can go".

As I came out I wondered how many more of such wasted days were in store for me and what course the case would take before the verdict was pronounced, removing one more complaint from the pending list.

37

FASHION FANTASIES

When I took a piece of cloth to my tailor for stitching a pair of trousers he asked me "Should I make a baggy?"

"Baggy!" I exclaimed.

"Yes a baggy," he repeated. "This is what in vogue these days".

Not sure of how a "baggy" looks like, I asked him to show one already stitched. Narrow at the bottoms and somewhat loose in the middle, it looked similar to what the matinee idol Dev Anand used to wear in his hey days.

I had a quick glance of the clothes hung in the show window. The safaris have become simple—no frills, extra shining buttons, etc. The trousers are now narrower at the bottoms (not the drain-pipe type we used to have three decades ago). The bell-bottoms, nick-named as brooms, was nowhere to be seen. Like bell-bottoms, double-breast suits, sola and felt hats, bows etc. are no more in fashion. They have been replaced by three-piece suits and the casual wears like jeans, T-shirts and bush shirts.

Coming back to film stars, I still remember how the youngsters were crazy to pattern their hair-styles to that of Dilip Kumar. Similarly, Sadhana-cut hair-style remained popular among school and college going girls for a long time. Sadhana could also be credited for popularising kurta-payjama among the womenfolk especially the teenagers. Raj Kapoor's *Awaara* type trousers (an ankle-up bottom) too caught up with the youngsters for a year or so but could not last long.

Like filmstars, the politicians too prefer to have their own style of outfits and appearances. The Gandhi cap was very popular both with the young and old during the freedom struggle days. The Nehru jacket was another distinct outfit that became popular with people of all age groups. Rajiv Gandhi's style of wearing shawl across the shoulders also caught up with many initially but could not find much favour later on. The Jodhpuri coat, though an undeclared official dress, has not been able to find favour either with the young or the old.

The French-cut beards have not been able to impress the Indians. After the late K.M. Pannikar, who used to sport a French-cut beard, others to follow him are I.K. Gujral, Jagdish Tytler and Sam Patrioda. Chandra Shekhar was another politician who looked different with a trimmed full-grown beard.

Probably the designers and creators of fashions keep the womenfolk in view while creating new fashions, because in their case only the trends change fast, whether the clothes or hair styles. If one day it is the salwar-kameez in vogue, the other day it may be lungi-kurta. The variety of hair styles as one sees these days is indicative of the fact that pigtails, plaits and even hair rolled into buns, are things of the past.

But it seems it is in the domain of the jewellery where designs change every day, if not every hour, compelling women, both young and old, to go in for new designs, notwithstanding the high cost of the yellow metal and very sparing use of it.

But one thing is certain that so long as individuals remain concerned about their appearances and outfits, fashion designers and creators will always be in demand.

38

CAUGHT NAPPING

I wish the English doctors who have discovered that there is a "lull" in the levels of alertness in human beings between 1 p.m. and 4 p.m. should have conducted studies in India before coming to any conclusion.

For the Indians any hour of the day is a "lull" time. Whether it is the breakfast or supper time, they fall into a slumber in a matter of seconds. In a way they prove right the learned doctors that day-napping is not connected with one's sleep during the night.

The place is also no bar for the Indians. Whether travelling in a crowded city bus, a train or an airline jet, they can simply go to sleep (sometimes very sound), in a twitch of an eye. Similarly whether it is the office, shop or factory, nobody can stop the habitual nappers.

There are some who can "steal" naps at any time of the day. The hustle and bustle and happenings around make no difference to them.

There are some who can switch on and off in regard to their naps. One moment they may be listening attentively, but the very next moment one might find them napping, notwithstanding the seriousness of the subject under discussion.

Then there are nappers who cannot resist sleep after the meals. They feel drowsy as soon as they finish their meals, no matter they are acting as hosts or are honoured guests.

But the most irritating about the nappers is that when travelling as co-passengers they fall on and even rest their heads on others' shoulders. And in case one protests, they feel bad and give a nasty look.

However, the learned doctors have a word of cheer for all those who nap during the day. "Do not feel guilty," they say "because there is nothing wrong with you." Probably they are right. Only those who suffer from insomnia and take sleeping pills to snatch a few minutes of sleep can vouch for it.

But in a way day-napping is a blessing in disguise. The nappers see no evil, hear no evil and speak no evil—three golden rules to lead a care-free life. But above all napping provides an opportunity to day dream.

39

ONE MAN DIED

A thud in one of the corners of a high-rise building under construction brought hordes of people to the site. A worker in his late-thirties had fallen from the seventh floor and met an instant death.

There was weeping and wailing by some of his comrades, especially the women. The site-manager came running and shouted: “Get aside, let me check”. He came close to the man lying flat on the floor and felt his pulse. “Call his wife. She is working on fourth floor,” he said.

The work had come to a standstill. The workers collected near the dead man and started shouting slogans against the site-manager and the building contractor. The site-manager left the place saying that he would inform the Saab and the police. The wailing, weeping and slogan shouting continued and reached its crescendo when the deceased’s wife arrived on the scene.

Unmindful of wailing and weeping, about a dozen persons sitting at a close-by tea-stall continued to sip tea and nibble at the snacks.

The contractor came in his air-conditioned Maruti, followed by siren-sounding ambulance and police jeep. None obstructed the contractor and the policemen. “Take him to the ambulance”, said one of the cops. The body was lifted and put in the ambulance and driven away. “There will not be any work today,” announced the contractor. The crowd started melting. Some continued to talk in whispers and hush-hush tones.

"Are you not insured?" someone who was heard asking a slogan shouting worker. The query was met with a stony silence.

Meanwhile the site-manager had arranged for tea and snacks for the workers. None refused. The children rather enjoyed the feast.

The slogan-shouting had ceased. Hissing hiccups had replaced the wailing and weeping.

"We will take you all to the cremation ground," informed the site manager. "Saab had already given money to make all the arrangements." There were mild protests, but he ignored them.

All this had happened at nine in the morning. By six in the evening everything looked normal. Even the chalk-markings of the police had disappeared.

"Has he been cremated?" I asked a worker who was very active in the morning. "Yes," he replied in a matter-of-fact tone. "Everything is settled".

"Settled?" I repeated.

"Yes everything is settled," he said emphatically. "Saab is kind enough to give five thousand rupees to the deceased's wife and has promised to provide a job to his ten-year-old son."

I was shocked and felt sorry for the little boy who would be carrying the bricks and mortar at such a tender age.

40

TIPSY TURVY

I think those who drink and get tipsy should be looked upon sympathetically. After all, a person in a tipsy frame of mind should be excused for the occasional oddity he may be inclined to indulge in. I hold this view, having viewed many such a person from the sidelines.

There is a colleague, who, without fail, sniffs out a get-together where liquor is being served and gets tipsy after a peg or two. Being the bucolic type, he starts abusing every-one present, even his superiors. But the very next day he makes amends by seeking apologies. He is forgiven.

A friend starts singing half-way through his peg sessions. All he requires is a victim around to listen to his songs. Most people avoid him like the plague, but once he catches hold of somebody, it is not easy to get away. Any interruption or reluctance to listen can invite his wrath. He thinks his voice is akin to K L Saigal's. The best way to get rid of him is to compare his voice with that of a singer other than Saigal.

I know another gentleman who starts reciting ghazals after a drink or two, but is at his best when he has had his full quota. Surprisingly he is not able to recite a single couplet when sober.

By and large the best-behaved drinkers are the services people. They rarely go beyond their quotas or the limits of good behaviour. The only occupational hazard of standing next to some of these is that they are given to talking tall after they have consumed their permitted quota of pegs.

I know of a retired army man who bores his listeners to death with his talk of the action he has seen in service. Any impatience or incredibility is sure to bring a rebuff from him. "You cannot appreciate all this because you think wars are won by pressing triggers only", he shoots back at those who belittle or refuse to believe his stirring sagas. Some listeners have found a way out. They get him another drink and he starts drooping.

The most feared alcoholic of all, however, has to be the belligerent kind who on one pretext or the other creates nasty scenes. The best thing to do is to ignore this kind, but sometimes indifference is as provocative as retaliation.

Take the case of yet another friend, a mild bespectacled gent who couldn't say boo to a goose when sober. A drink or two and he turns into a belligerent fiend, accusing everybody of staring at his wife (a mousy little thug) and his wife, of staring at everybody. If that doesn't work he gets violent over the amount of ice in his drink. The next morning he is humbly contrite, his face shining with sincerity and his spectacles neatly in place.

And then there are the ones, who start out the life and soul of the party to turn into maudlin wet blankets.

Many of these confess to their guilt and their acts of commission or omission after their bouts. But there are those who conveniently say they don't remember a thing, leaving others with the option of either learning to forget and forgive or to grind their teeth helplessly and clean up the mass.

Although no party can be termed a success without one or more of any of these kinds, the ones I admire most are those who remain exactly as they were when they first walked in. Their talk undergoes no sudden change, their walk remains as steady as a straight line and no invitation is required for them to say Encyclopedia Brittanica without giving way to the knees.

41

BACKDOOR ENTRIES

We paint our front doors, embellish them with ornate brass handles and place welcome mats before them to ensure our guests of our hospitality, our status in life. Our front doors then are the very symbol of the fronts we preserve, like our carefully painted smiles and immaculate ties.

The backdoor, on the other hand, is rarely looked after. Rusty padlocks keep them closed, if not the rubbish that accumulates over time in every household. These doors are 'decorated' with armless, bottomless chairs, broken children's toys, old newspapers and other domestic debris.

Like our front doors, our care extends itself to the roads and lanes they face. Pavements are reconstructed, trees are planted and facelifts given at every opportunity to prove our worthiness. And like our backdoors, the lanes they face reflect the dirt piled up within. Dirt that spills over into these lanes, in the form of carelessly flung garbage.

Every rear lane looks the same, whether it lies in West End or Wazirabad, chocked with garbage, overflowing drains and the residue from houses bordering it. Even the annual cleaning, whether it is for a politician's visit or because the residents finally cannot bear the stench any more, makes little difference. The very people who painstakingly polish their front doors, treat their rear entrances with shabby contempt.

And yet, it is in these backlanes that the best *dhabas*, with their mouthwatering food, the tea-stalls with prompt service and the car and scooter workshops are found. In residential colonies, other lifesavers are to be seen, working industriously at ironing or sorting out old piles of paper and bottles, chores that relieve the housewife of some of her burden and bring in a little extra income.

Part-time maids come through these entrances and deals are struck here exchanging old clothes for new steel utensils. As much as we neglect these byelanes, we use them to further our own ends.

The ends do not stop at the back door stoop. We use other back-doors to gain entrance for our children to schools and colleges. Airline and train reservations are made through these entrances when the front door has been slammed in our faces. By knocking on these doors we bring the filth of the byelanes behind our houses to them, in the bribes and crooked deals that are given and taken.

Politicians use backdoor tactics to malign their opponents, when they can't find the dirt on their 'fronts'. And backdoor diplomacy is far more successful these days than the straight approach.

The backdoor has been most useful to all those who indulge in deals on the shadier side of the law. Smugglers, hoarders and anti-social elements much prefer to operate through this entrance, with the understanding if not the collusion of those who are supposed to curb these activities. What is not available in the market, can be had by surreptitiously entering or knocking at the door of the lane behind it.

Of course there are those who are not aware of the existence of these doors. These are the people who continue to wait in queues, sit interminably in lobbies and at reception counters in the hope that their turn will come. Either they have no knowledge of how things are done or they refuse to have anything to do with those who open these doors at the rustle of money or the whispering of a slip with a big name written on it.

But these are few and far between, for, for each one that dumps his refuse neatly in the right place, there are ten who would rather pitch it anywhere, for others to clean up the mess.

42

TRULY YOURS

I am of the firm opinion that the bosses and seniors "become" what we make of them.

Flatter them and they feel elated. Pamper them and they feel pleased. In fact, it is the juniors who spoil them and raise their expectations, and any laxity on their part invites the wrath of the seniors and bosses.

I know of many bosses and 'high-ups' who claim that they do not encourage "sycophancy", but at the same time do not mind having "chamchas" around them, and fully depend on them.

There are many a gentleman who keep a calendar of the dates of birth not only of their bosses and seniors but also of their spouses and children and never forget to send their greetings, and of course, the gifts.

There are some who get "briefed" about the good habits—both likes and dislikes—and their preferred brands of cigarettes, wines, scents, perfumes, colognes, etc. of their bosses and invariably 'cater' to their 'tastes', whenever an occasion comes their way, or very often 'create' occasion to get close to their bosses and seniors.

For them it is an investment for earning 'dividends' in future.

That the 'homecoming' of a wayward son could be an occasion for celebration was demonstrated by a friend of mine who has mastered the art of keeping himself on the right side of his bosses. And there were many who "obliged" him by gracing the occasion.

The gentleman made full use of the presence of the persons who mattered and when the time came to fix up the son, he succeeded and got him a coveted job.

To some, the festivals come very handy to promote sycophancy. They make it a point to take gifts to their bosses, be it a Diwali, an Onam (if the boss hails from Kerala), or a Pongal (if the senior is a Tamilian).

These days to send only the cards is considered to be an outdated mode of greeting. The cards may not even register the names of the senders in the minds of those who are being greeted. One has to hammer one's identity for future encashment.

But the sycophancy does pay. I know of many "good-for-nothing" fellows who got promotions and reached the top positions, just because they have perfected the art of keeping their bosses and seniors in good humour.

In due course they have also learnt the art of keeping at bay all those who are likely to be their competitors.

But at the same time there are many upright persons who hate to join the rat race and refuse to become the "yes men".

43

OF MATCHES AND MATCH-MAKING

The occasional arguments between the lady of the house and the younger daughter have many a time enlivened an otherwise somewhat quiet atmosphere of the house.

Sunday morning and holidays are really the ones that upset my wife. In her anxiety to clear the backlog that piles up during the week, she is seen handling not one but at least half-a-dozen chores at a time. I being of no use to her, she wants the younger one to get up and lend a helping hand. But her pleadings with her fall on deaf ears. She does not even stir in her bed, leave alone responding to her mother's repeated pleas.

The other irritant that annoys the senior lady to no end is the way the younger one, who is now college going, maintains her room. Nothing is found in order there. Rarely she bothers to keep her belongings—clothes, books, contents of the cupboards, etc.—in a tidy manner.

Both these habits of the younger one have very often antagonized her mother. The later holds the view that taking active interest in the kitchen work and starting an early day stand in good stead for a girl when it comes to finalizing a match for her.

But I do not think so and the lady of the house should know it better because these two issues were not even remotely raised by either side when I had okayed the proposal and accepted her as my bride.

However, it was not so about half-a-century ago. I vividly remember my mother telling us that in her days not only the probing questions used to be asked about the girls' habits but they were also asked to cook meals and serve to the prospective grooms and those who accompanied them. Of course, there were many to help them and grooms' parties could easily be bluffed. But some canny ladies accompanying the grooms used to have third eye to expose such bluffs.

Yet another way to impress the grooms and their parents was to exhibit before them *works* of embroidery supposed to have been done by the girls. Engravings like "good night", "welcome", etc. on pillow-covers and "flowers", "parrots", "sparrows", "peacocks", and other such figurative works on the bedsheets used to be features of the "craftsmanship".

But the times seem to have changed. The advent of the gadgets like micro-waves, dishwashers, washing machines, juicers, mixies, etc. and easy availability of ready-to-cook stuff, have made all the old forms of matrimonial negotiations irrelevant.

None is bothered to know as to at what time the girl gets up or how good she is at cooking or what sort of embroidery work she can undertake.

These days while the youngsters talk of fast-food restaurants, pop music, etc. their elders evince interest only in their respective moveable and immoveable properties. And above all there are computers to assist them in the task of match-making.

44

MUCH-MALIGNED MAMASHREES

When at a marriage reception my sister's son called from a distance, there was a derisive laughter from many a corner.

"Mamaji, will you come here, please? I want to talk to you urgently."

"Go, 'Mamashree' go," a voice interrupted,

"Duryodhan wants to have some advice from you."

Again there was a laughter, this time almost everybody joining in it. I took all this sportingly. Any protest would have invited more comments.

The maternal uncles are really in very poor spot these days, and it is all because of 'Mama Kansa' and 'Mama Shakuni' the latter in particular.

'Mahabharat' apart, even in many a Hindi movie, the maternal uncles have been portrayed in a bad light. Like Shakuni, they are shown interfering in the lives of their sisters and wrecking the peace of their homes. However, the uncles invariably get exposed and humiliated, though the fact remains that they have in mind only the welfare of their sisters, nephews and nieces.

But why blame the Mamas alone? The nephews and nieces can also get nasty. They can be as crooked and scheming or alternatively as honest and helpful as their uncles. Same can also be said about 'chachas' and 'bhatijas'. But surprisingly, there is no tale-telling about them.

I have no idea about the sort of relationships maternal uncles maintain with their nephews in other parts of India. But in the State I come from, the 'bhanjas' are held in great esteem by their 'mamas'. Rather, at times, the nephews are accorded VIP treatment. At the time of their marriages, the 'mamas' are supposed to give not only special gifts but also perform certain 'ceremonies' (involving quite an expenditure) which they do ungrudgingly.

Unlike Shakuni of 'Mahabharat' or the maternal uncles of Hindi movies, it is very rare that the 'Mamas' go and stay with their married sisters. Rather, they get immense pleasure in having the sisters at their homes and extending all possible hospitality, sometimes even going out of their way.

But probably, the damage is already done. 'Mamas' may not be able to refurbish their image so long as 'Mahabharat' is fresh in the memories of the people. But if sisters are going to act like 'Gandharis', the 'Mamas' are doomed forever.

45

NOT STATIC

As I look around I find that a teenager of today is not what he or she used to be, say, three or four decades ago. A sea change is discernible.

The type of freedom a teenager enjoys these days was never there for us. Whether it was the choice of outfits (I got my first pair of trousers when I entered the college) or hair-styles, the seniors used to decide for us. But these days the elders are only asked if not ordered, to get stitched clothes for the youngsters as per the prevailing fashion.

In our teenage days the parents used to select movies (all the movies were not considered fit for our viewing) for us. But thanks to the invasion of DVDs the youngsters now view all the movies without any inhibition. Rather they decide what movies the seniors should view.

In this age of electronics media it might be beyond one's imagination that a medium wave receiving set used to be considered a luxury till the mid-forties, and we used to "steal" moments to listen to the film music and radio plays. But now with the wide choice of audio and video cassettes, CDs and DVDs, the teenagers enjoy the film and other music to their hearts' content, and that too without anybody questioning or interrupting them.

The teenagers of today should consider themselves lucky for being spared of elders' sermons. For us there were many 'dos' and 'don'ts'; and we used to be taken to task for any violation.

The type of discipline we had experienced is nowhere to be seen these days. Even whistling around in the house (especially in the company of ladies) was forbidden and frowned upon and at times brought reprimands. But these days elders glee and grin and give rhythmic claps when youngsters dance with music being played on the stereophonic sound system.

The elders and seniors used to be the final arbitrators and decision makers in the matrimonial matters. Boy approving a girl or a girl okaying a boy never formed a part of the negotiations. But these days the seniors just standby as the youngsters decide about their life partners. The elders only play a role when matters relating dowry, etc. are to be settled.

However, language of romance has undergone no change during all these years. A modern Romeo still compared his Julliet with moon, though he knows well that the moon is not what a Romeo of fifties used to imagine. Similarly the Julliet of today continues to talk sweet nothings, forgetting the hard realities of life that loom large beyond the realms of romance. But a lover of today is certainly more defiant and determined as compared with the one of yesteryears.

However, I admire the teenagers of today for just one reason. The type of competition they face, whether it is admission to the school and college or securing a job, we never confronted. It is really heart-breaking experience for them.

It is quite possible that in the new century the scenario may altogether be different from what we observe now; because time and tide never remain static.

46

SAHIB, SWAGATAM

A new boss was on the way. Who would he (She? no never!) be? That was what weighed on everybody's mind. Guesses were made. Some mentioned certain names on "authoritative basis". Some circulated other names on the basis of "inside information". Some "floated" certain names keeping in view their own vested interests and those of the present boss.

When at last the rumours were set at rest, everybody was taken by surprise. The new incumbent was a dark horse in the real sense; he was not even remotely connected with our organisation at any time.

The announcement created problems for all those who had indulged in name-dropping. Hastily they twisted their statements, condemning in the process all those persons whose names they had circulated. As a further cover-up they praised the new boss with all the force at their command.

Meanwhile, the "seasoned" diplomats of the office got busy assembling the "bio-data" of the incoming boss. Place of birth, mother-tongue, ancestry, kith, kin and in-laws, education, previous experience and of course: "How did he manage to get the post?" "What sort of connections he has with those who have selected him for the post?" And in a week or so an up-to-date dossier was ready on the gentleman.

The "careerists" went right to work on the new boss from Day One. They wasted no time in "holding responsible" the outgoing boss for all the "mess" organisation was in. In the same breath, they talked of the virtues of the new boss and to prove their point quoted extensively from "the facts" they had painstakingly gathered.

The arrival of the new boss infused new life in all those who for years were "ignored"—or at least felt themselves ignored. They too jumped into the fray with a hope that the wind might blow on their side also. Their toughest competition came from those who had weathered many a boss. Most were outmanoeuvred and compelled to fall back into the grooves they were trying to emerge from.

For those who had helplessly watched all these developments from the sidelines and believed in the policy of "wait and watch", the situation never changed. They continued to wring their hands without being called to the arena.

Days passed. The new boss was no more new and things settled down leaving the field to all those who had perfected the art of "tackling" new bosses. Once again they had complete control over the situation, if not the boss.

47

NEW YEAR CARDS

Unlike many I have never been too eager to send New Year greeting cards to friends, relations, bosses and other acquaintances. I consider it to be a luxury. Apart from the cost of cards (good cards are very costly these days), there is an additional expense of postage (one just cannot hand over a card; it has to be sent by post or courier service).

However, there are many who are very enthusiastic about sending cards and plan well in advance. But at the same time there are some who consider the whole exercise a necessary evil and undertake it very grudgingly.

There are some who may not be in touch with others all round the year but find it very convenient to renew their contacts through the greeting cards. It is yet another way to tell the world that they are alive and kicking.

For those who hold high positions sending greeting cards is no problem for them. Their offices do the needful. They can afford to be liberal and may include their kith and kin (probably the best way to publicise the post one is holding). Even the staff attached to these persons profit by the practice.

Some get their quota (depending on the position they hold) of greeting cards from their offices, but are required to spend on postage.

Then we have those who are very selective in sending the cards. They prefer to greet only those who really matter to them. For example, a businessman may not forget to greet an ITO or a STC.

Similarly, an assistant awaiting his promotion will send the best available card to his officer (and make it a point to greet the spouse also) who is to write his annual confidential report.

I, however, appreciate those—and they constitute the majority—who spend on the cards. They take the trouble of going to the market and take pains in selecting the cards keeping in view the person they intend to greet (Should one take it that they are the only genuine well-wishers?).

However, there are some who wait till the last week or even the last day of the year, to buy the cards. The "left-overs", as they are called, are certainly cheaper. The only drawback in this is that the best of the stuff is not available.

It may sound strange but true that there are some who reuse the cards (especially the ones which do not carry the number of the year) received by them a year or two ago, though they take care to make some minor changes here and there. Frankly speaking, I find nothing wrong in it because greetings are greetings, whether sent through an expensive card or a reused one. What matters is the sincerity of the sender.

48

TRUCKS TO ANYWHERE

On my morning walks I invariably found three trucks, at times even four, parked near the slums inhabited by about 20,000 people. Summer or winter, spring or autumn, torrential rains or biting cold, these trucks arrived on the dot at 5.30 a.m. near a tea-stall. Each vehicle had two attendants besides the driver.

Every day I saw hundreds of men, women (many carrying babes in their arms) and children (including toddlers and tiny-tots), all from the slums, being herded into these trucks, each carrying more than hundred and odd persons. The majority were always underclothed and barefoot. Even on the coldest and foggy days I found most of them inadequately clothed.

Most of them, especially the women, carried in their hands *chappatis* wrapped in not-so-clean pieces of rags. They must have got up quite early to make them, though they perhaps put in the same hours and the amount of work as did the men.

It was probably my curiosity that prompted me to reach the spot little early one day and talk to some of them. "Where do these trucks take you to?" I asked the one whom I had seen almost everyday.

"No fixed place," he replied. "One day it may be to Vasant Kunj, another day to some construction site in Noida or Ghaziabad, and yet another day to Gurgaon or Yamuna Paar."

"Who decides?"

"That man there," he replied and pointed towards a man who was sipping tea in the tea-stall. As I was talking to him some more had joined him.

"Are the same persons taken every day?"

"No. It again depends on that man," he said and added, "To keep him in good humour we supply him wine every night and at times women also."

"Who pays your wages and how much do you get for a day's work?"

"That man gives us our wages and we accept whatever he gives." This time another man replied to my question. "Did you ever protest for getting less than what you deserved?" Another man intervened to say, "Then he will never take us again and also tell other contractors not to hire us."

"Why do you take your kids along with you?"

"To save them from drug traffickers and addicts."

"Why don't you send them to school?"

A somewhat oldish man intervened to say, "The construction sites are schools and bricks are books for them."

"How much are you paid?" I asked a woman. "Only my *mard* knows," she replied. "Most of the women are accompanied by their husbands," a woman volunteered.

I observed that all the time I was talking to these people, their eyes travelled occasionally to the tea-stall where "that man" sat. Suddenly he got up and came to me and shouted, "What are you doing here?" Before I could say anything he added threateningly, "Now go away and don't be seen here anymore." Then he warned those talking to me not to talk to "strangers".

Even after a week trucks continued to come, though they were now parked at a little distance from the tea-stall. The sturdy man was on his job everyday but was accompanied by a policeman. But I did not anymore see the man who did most of the talking to me. I felt a little guilty.

49

FILLING IN A FORM

I do not know about others, but I feel very ill at ease whenever I am asked to fill in a form. Not that I am not capable of undertaking the task, it is usually the details that one is required to provide, and the spaces earmarked for them, that irritate me. I always find it to be a taxing job.

But it seems there is no escape because the forms and the form-filling procedure have become an inseparable part of our life. Be it the making of a ration card (an Indian's 'green card' in other words); or applying for jobs, passports and licences of different types and their renewal; be it the filling of sales-tax and income-tax returns; reserving seats for rail and bus journeys; or admitting of one's wards to educational institutions, filling forms is a must.

However, it is a different matter whether anybody goes into the information so painstakingly provided by the applicants. Probably none cares, unless of course, an element of mischief is involved or some action is needed to be taken against the one submitting the form. I am, however, of the firm view that most of the details are superfluous irrelevant and serve no purpose.

The most irritating aspect of the filling in exercise is the 'spaces' provided for the information desired. The space wherein one is asked to write the name in 'capital' letters is barely enough to write one's surname! At times it may not be possible to write the 'initials' of 'first' and 'second' names, leave alone names in 'full' and 'block' letters. Similarly, the columns and spaces for the addresses, including pin codes, are very often good enough for writing house and block numbers, and one may have to insert a "hyphen" while writing the names of one's town or city (it's worse in cases requiring the name of the village complete with tehsil, taluk and district). The classical examples are of the money order and railway reservation forms.

At times the spaces allotted for writing amounts, in words, can accommodate only two or three-digit numerals. One may have to carry the other digit—figures and paise to another place and indicate via an arrow!

Yet another complication in regard to forms, is the numbers; very often prefixed with some alphabets, they are usually associated with. Unless one is well-versed with the numbers, it may be difficult to lay one's hands on the right form. One has to visit the vendor who sells forms for filling of income-tax and sales tax returns, and know the types and categories of the forms one may be required to fill in for the purpose.

That the forms have become a profit-making proposition can be deduced from the fact that one may be asked to pay rupees 10 for a single sheet form, although its cost of production is less than 10 paise.

All said and done, I hold the view that instead of making the forms simple and straight, they are steadily getting more and more complicated with every passing day.

Probably we Indians are being subjected to some sort of an I.Q. test through these exercises.

50

FROM TABLE TO CABLE

Babu Ram, who runs a hair-cutting saloon and whom I am patronising for the past two decades or so, started his business with just one table, and that too, a wooden one with no sunmica top and other frills. It used to have one drawer which was meant both for keeping tools and the day's earnings. To supplement his income Babu Ram had let-out three-fourths of his shop to an electrician and kept to himself only a corner.

Very few people visited Babu Ram's shop. (None was prepared to call it a *saloon*). "It is better to go to a man who runs his business under a tree" said many about Babu Ram's shop. I started patronising him because he did a good job.

After about two years or so, the electrician was asked to vacate the place. The shop was re-done with two more tables added to it. All the tables had blue sunmica tops (matching with the colour of the distemper), each having different drawers for stacking tools and earnings and other knick-knacks. Babu Ram recruited two more persons to assist him. He started keeping a Hindi daily and backdated movie magazines to keep his customers entertained as they waited for their turn. A radio, which always remained tuned in to the Vividh Bharati, was also added. An air-cooler for summers and a room heater for winters were the other assets which Babu Ram very often used to mention to his customers whose number had increased substantially by then.

Then came the Sunday morning serial "Ramayana" and Babu Ram immediately got installed a black-and-white television set. When the "Mahabharat" went on the air, he replaced the B&W

set with a colour one. On my suggestion, he also started getting an English daily. Meanwhile, he increased his rates by about one hundred per cent. But no one grudged or protested. Rather his clientele continued to grow.

The best thing about Babu Ram is that he is very receptive to suggestions and ideas, provided it helps him in getting more customers. That was probably the reason that when I suggested to him to get his television set hooked on to the Cable TV, he lost no time in doing so; and it did make a lot of difference to his business.

"Now the customers walk in at any hour of the day and get themselves updated with the world news through the BBC as I do my job", he told me.

But one thing which has really surprised me about Babu Ram is his outfits. He used to wear Safaris initially; then switched over to the shirts and jeans; and now wears spotless white kurta-payjamas: though I feel the order should have been the other way round.

"Why don't you wear shirts, jeans and safaris any more?" I asked him recently.

"Because only men with kurta-payjamas become netas," he was quick to reply and added, "and I would not like to miss an opportunity whenever it comes my way". I was inclined to agree with him.

51

NOBLE SENTIMENTS!

I am thinking of leaving a Will in which, apart from making many observations and assertions (which may not be of any consequence), I am going to indicate that my body be handed over to doctors for undertaking any research on it, so that it may be of some use to mankind in future. By doing so, I am trying to emulate a gentleman who two decades ago had taken the same decision and was lauded by the then Prime Minister.

However, I am certain that many including some dear and near ones, are not going to look upon this (my resolve) very kindly.

Imagine the plight of the friends and foes who have been eagerly looking forward to the day when they would be asked to join the funeral procession and become pall-bearers. The cherished desire of the one who (I am not sure who he or she may be) is to light my pyre may remain unfulfilled. Even those who are waiting to wail and weep (especially those adept in shedding crocodile tears) might be disappointed.

The *acharaj* (pandit who performs the last rites) and the shopkeeper who makes both ends meet by selling coffins, will also curse me for depriving them of their usual income.

As the ashes will not be taken to Haridwar for immersion in the Ganga, the *pandas*, who wait for years to do their 'rightful' duty to the departed soul, will also feel dejected.

My forefathers whose names are buried in the *bahais* (the red books maintained by the *pandas*) will not look down kindly from the heavens (heaven or hell, I am not very sure?) for the 'break' in the records of the family history. The future generations will also curse me when they will not find my name in the *bahais* of the *pandas*.

The greatest disappointment in store probably will be for the *pandits*, who are treated to feasts during *sharads*, I am sure they will not only shower abuse on me, but also spit on my heirs.

As my body will not be subjected to the prescribed rites, there is every possibility that I may not attain *moksh* (that is, salvation) and my *atma* (soul) might wander disturbing the peace of foes who must have heaved a sigh of relief after my death, but at the same time consoling those who would be cherishing my memories: the hypocrites!

However, I fear that before the execution of my Will, many including my kith and kin, may declare me mentally unsound, and, without bothering about my Will, do exactly what customs and traditions demand.

52

DEATH OF A PARK

Not long ago there was a beautiful park in our neighbourhood, and, if I recall correctly, it was inaugurated by the then Lt. Governor with all the pomp and show that usually go with such functions. Well-laid beds of flowers of all varieties and species; lawns with plush green grass; and rows of tree plantations were some of the features, which used to attract many morning strollers to it. A children's park with swings and see-saws was another attraction for kids of all age-groups.

But the park is now no more. I have seen its slow and steady decay.

It all started when the local authorities decided to reserve one-fourth of the park for receptions and other parties connected with marriages. Frequent erection of *pandals* and *shamianas* not only destroyed the flowers and plants, but also left many a gaping hole in the lawn ruling out any further growth of blades of grass. This portion of the park is now a barren piece of land.

Every alternate day it is littered with heaps of used *donas* and crumbs of food and other left-overs which stink for days together without anybody (not even the ones who spend lakhs on the receptions) caring to clean it, till, of course, it is time for another show.

Then one day I saw the children of a primary school, housed in a nearby bungalow across the road, holding their morning prayer assembly and the PT classes in the park. It is now more or less the playground of the school and the Principal very proudly announces this fact to all those who come to seek admission for their wards.

Half of the park was thus out of bounds for the regular users. They thanked the encroachers for sparing the other half for their use. However, it was a short-lived dream. The organisers of Diwali and New Year eve melas and Jagrans started using the portion adjoining the one being used for marriages. As of now, it seems that this portion will remain earmarked for holding such shows.

As one encroacher after another was on the job, a *Panditji* came from nowhere and installed an idol of Lord Shiva in one of the corners and encircled it with a *pucca* structure. He invited a local politician for the *Murti Sansthapan* ceremony, thus ensuring that none dared demolish it.

As if all these encroachments were not enough to "kill" the park, the portion or whatever was left, has now been allotted to a 'public school' (owned by a local prominent political leader), ironically named "Rainbow". Trucks have been already unloading bricks and other building material. Very soon a concrete structure would be coming up at a place which not long ago was a beautiful park.

53

RELIVING PAST THROUGH JUNK

Diwali cleanings and clearances are not an annual fixture with us. These exercises are undertaken only when it becomes impossible to stand the sight of the overflowing junk, and dirt and dust start giving one a feeling of nausea. This year a similar situation had arisen, compelling us to go through the ordeal.

All the 'condemned' items (they could be useful for some) were got together, and I was assigned the taxing task of sorting them out.

Among the lot, was a trunkful of some old books, Press-clippings and photographs. As I was in the process of dusting the stuff, my eyes got suddenly rivetted on a group photograph taken at the time of the send-off to the students of the Intermediate class (popularly known as F.Sc.) in the college. As I concentrated on different faces in this keepsake photograph, I was reminded of many incidents associated with some of them.

In the row where teachers and the principal were seated, I could immediately spot always-in-a-good-mood lecturer in Physics, Mr Jagat Narain who later became an air ace in the Indian Air Force and, if I remember aright, was mentioned handsomely in despatches during the 1965 Indo-Pak war. Unfortunately, he died near Bangalore while doing a test-run for the MiG-21 in the mid '70s, thus cutting short what could have been a splendid career.

I also spotted the love lorn and always wearing the 'Devdas' looks teacher of English, Mr Manmohan Kalia (a short-story writer and literary figure in his own right).

Then I spotted our music lecturer, one Mr Upadhya. The poor man could never fulfil his ambition of singing on All India Radio, notwithstanding the numerous audition tests he was asked to appear for: "You need connections to get assignments on AIR," he used to tell the students. I little understood the meaning of the word connections at that time. But now that I do, my heart goes out to a man who was really talented.

The rest of the staff were serious, the over-studious type who never mingled with students.

Among the students was Madan Lal, the "Mohammed Rafi" of our college. He had a very good voice, and made repeated rounds of Bombay to try his luck as a playback singer, but every time he returned dejected. Immediately after appearing for the examinations, he once again left for Bombay and was lost for ever. Later on I learnt that he had committed suicide.

In the corner of the last row stood the most brilliant student of our class and the college. He stood first in the university in the F.Sc. exams and continued thus in his career also. He is none else but Mr Yoginder Pal Anand, who retired as the Chairman of the Railway Board.

From among the girl students, who sat on the grass just in front of the teaching staff, Indira was the most extraordinary. Not only was she brilliant at her studies, but was also a great fighter of 'causes'. Unfortunately, she got herself entangled with a businessman's son who ditched her, the shock putting an end to the further studies of such a promising student; she left college before her graduation.

"How much time do you need to clear junk?" shrilly queried the lady of the house, breaking my train of reminiscences. Nevertheless, I had relived almost whole two years of my college life.

54

KHALNAYAKS AT THE HELM

That real life is altogether different from what one sees on the silver screen dawned on me recently, while travelling in a city bus.

Right from the moment a gang of four boarded the bus, it was clear that they were out to create mischief. They started indulging in all sorts of talk and antics.

They refused to buy tickets and told the conductor that they always travelled free, and no conductor had the guts to challenge them.

They embarrassed a young couple engaged in intimate talk by making some suggestive gestures and remarks. One of the gangsters teased a young girl, and, when she protested, she was told that if she was so touchy she should travel in a taxi. The girl chose to keep mum. But, when an old man made a feeble protest he was told to mind his own business.

Not only this, they then made sarcastic remarks about a girl who was engrossed in a book. "Baby, don't strain your beautiful eyes. They are not meant for these silly black alphabets." Though the girl ignored them, a young man, who objected to their remark, was told, "Why are you bothered about her? Is she your mother?" The shocked youngman could hardly mumble a few words of protest.

I wished some courageous man would pick up strength to take on the gangsters and teach them a lesson. But there was no one. I was itching to talk (taking them on physically was beyond me) to them, but could not pick up the courage to do so. I was afraid they would insult me also. Moreover, they needed bashing and not a dose of reasoning.

They continued with their obscene and vulgar running commentary, like they do in our Hindi movies. But the celluloid hero fights half-a-dozen goons and throws them out of the running bus. His deed is appreciated by co-passengers and the victim.

But how even the celluloid world stands degenerated. With *khalnayaks* ruling the roost, the heroes have to keep shut!

And I kept shut, too, though against my conscience.

55

MUNDANE PROBLEMS: SWAMI'S REMEDIES

It was the summer of 1959. It was one of those rare occasions when Swami Chinmayananda had agreed to grant private audience to some of those who had been attending his discourses on Bhagwad Gita in the Bapu Samaj Kendra on Panchkuian Road in New Delhi. I vividly remember it was one of the ante-rooms of the Sadan where he met us and spoke.

"You only generalise the things in your discourses which hardly help an individual." I made this stupid statement, fearing wild reaction from Swamiji and others.

Swamiji looked towards me, gave a broad smile and talked in a low and measured tone: "Youngman, I am neither a soothsayer nor a *tantrik*. Nor do I possess occult powers. I am no super human-being either. Still in case you need my guidance, I am there to help you."

Many among his small audience felt encouraged and came forward with their problems and sought Swamiji's guidance.

A businessman said: "I am always under strain because of my business."

"What is your business?" asked Swamiji.

"I am manufacturing auto spare parts."

"Share your profits with your workers and work for their welfare, your tensions will automatically disappear." The businessman probably had not expected the sort of advice Swamiji had given him. He stood crest-fallen.

"My marital life is not very happy Swamiji," a young lady spoke haltingly.

"Have you tried to find out the reason?" asked Swamiji. The lady did not reply to Swamiji's query. Swamiji continued: "First do that and then talk to your husband. It is the mutual trust and frankness among the spouses that makes the marital life happy. If you are wrong admit it, and if he is at fault tell him."

There was a gentleman who wanted to know from Swamiji how should he tackle his two sons and their wives who did not care for him and his wife. "Just ignore them and spend more time in Bhagwad Gita and you will find yourself at peace," Swamiji advised him.

"I am a very short-tempered person. In fact I land myself in many a trouble because of my temper," I said somewhat hesitatingly and added. "Is there some way out?"

"Very simple," Swamiji sermonized. "Remove yourself from the scene, take a glass of water and start reciting *Hari Om.*"

I didn't believe that Swamiji's prescription could cure me from an ailment which I was carrying for years; but it did. I hope that others who had sought Swamiji's guidance on that day were benefitted by his advice.

56

THE TALE OF THE OLD TIFFIN-BOX

My wife had purchased a tiffin-box on the Diwali-eve about three decades ago. Ever since then it had been my companion to the office.

It has two air tight slots, one for vegetable or dal or curd and another for rice or *chappatis.* Notwithstanding some dents and scratches here and there, it still looks sleek and has almost the same shine, it had thirty years ago. Probably the manufacturers in those days were more quality-conscious and believed in using superior raw-material.

The tiffin-box has stood by me well all these years, and if I say, through thick and thin. It almost symbolises my career-graph.

For years I carried in it only *chappatis* and some pickles, never making use of the second slot. But as the things brightened up career-wise, its contents too got progressively better with *pulaos, kheer* and *raitas* of different varieties.

I still remember how initially I used to feel somewhat hesitant while opening my tiffin-box before my colleagues, leave alone sharing its contents with them. But later on not only I started sharing my tiffin with others, but also made it a point to announce occasionally that but for the size of the tiffin-box I could have brought one or two more 'dishes'. And I must say that the stuff I carried used to finish in a jiffy, but not before I had 'tasted' it to enable me to answer any possible queries from my wife about the food so painstakingly prepared by her.

I had altogether forgotten about the tiffin-box till the other day I heard my wife telling the younger daughter. "Now that your Papa is not taking his lunch in this tiffin-box anymore, why don't you start taking your lunch in it?"

"Me?" the daughter was quick to react. "Forget about it Mummy. You want me to carry that wretched thing to my office. No way. There is a very good fast-food restaurant near my office where one can get every type of stuff all through the day."

Pursuing the matter further would have been an exercise in futility.

57

ON BECOMING A 'BARATI'

Gone are probably the days when to be invited for a groom's marriage was considered to be a privilege. The groom's parents used to insist on your joining the marriage party and ensured that you were looked after well till the ceremonies were over.

But the things seem to have undergone a sea-change. These days you are just 'asked' to join the marriage party (barat) leaving entirely to your 'pleasure' whether to 'grace' the 'occasion' or not. The card distribution exercise is undertaken with an 'eye' on the 'shagoon' or gifts expected to be received to offset wholly or partially the marriage expenses.

Even if you are not able to attend the marriage, it is for you to ensure that you mark your presence by way of your 'shagoon' (minimum these days is five hundred rupees with no upper limit). But the irony is that your presence (in your best outfits and attires) also makes no difference, unless you are a person who 'matters'. Otherwise you are just one of those two hundred and odd 'baratis' (there is no limit on the number because it is all at the expense of bride's side) which accompany the groom. At times you may even be asked to reach the bride's place or the 'meeting point'.

The 'baratis' are almost herded into the buses (don't mind if a member of the band party is thrusting his drum or trumpet on your face) or cars (again depending on your status or equation you have with the groom or his parents). As the groom's parents are either attending to some ceremonies or performing 'bhangra' you are left to fend yourself.

After being dropped at the 'meeting point', you are made to walk and enjoy (per force) the out-of-step 'bhangra' performed by some tipsy youngsters, relations, friends, and of course, the parents of the groom. Time is no consideration.

Once inside the pandal at the bride's place, the 'baratis' are sure to lose their identity. One cannot differentiate between a 'barati' and the one belonging to the bride's side.

With eyes on watches and on that part of the pandal where the dinner is laid; the 'baratis' wait anxiously for the signal to 'invade' the dining tables. At times even this is not required. It is possible the guests of the bride's side adhering to the rule of 'first come, first served' may take their food even before the 'baratis' are signalled to go ahead. But the fear that you may not miss the last bus service or the bus which is to take the 'baratis' back, virtually keeps you on your toes and you may not be able to enjoy the best of the cuisines so painstakingly got prepared by the bride's side. You may regret for not recovering even partially the 'shagoon' or the money you have spent on your gift.

You try to locate groom's parents or make efforts to catch the groom's eye to convey your good wishes and thanks, but all in vain. They are all busy in 'giving takes' to the video cameraman. You only wave and take their leave.

Next time in case you are asked to become a barati, think twice.

58

PUNJABI "KUDI" DID IT!

"You seem to be a Punjabi," said a gentleman standing three steps behind me in the queue at the bus stop. I nodded though did feel somewhat offended. "That is why you are trying to jump the queue", the gentleman added, though I was trying to do nothing of the sort. I was only trying to ensure that those who stood ahead of me, the youngsters in particular, did not encourage infiltrators.

"Do only the Punjabis jump the queues?" I mused to myself. I have observed people jumping the queues at Mumbai, Bengaluru, Kolkata and Chennai, and I am sure, they were not all Punjabis. I had a mind to point this fact to the gentleman, but chose to keep mum. But I didn't like the manner he had "generalised" his observation. Surprisingly, no one in the queue reacted to his observation. "Maybe it is aimed at me only", I thought.

The bus came and, as usual, the queue was nowhere to be seen. The gentleman was almost the first to get in. By the time my turn came all the seats were occupied. I found myself standing near the seat where the gentleman sat.

"You see I didn't jump the queue", I said inviting his attention. He gave me a furious look. "You will agree with me that all the Punjabis are not the queue jumpers", I added to make my point. My observation was again met with a furious look and a glum face.

I had by then understood that the gentleman was certainly "cut up" with the Punjabis, and was not prepared to listen to anything said by way of an argument to rebut his observation.

This happened a year ago. But during thirty minutes' journey the gentleman's furious looks and glum face had got imprinted on my mind.

But recently when I came face to face with the same gentleman at my friend's son's marriage reception who introduced him as "Mr Gopalaswami, my colleague", I found him an altogether a changed person. I recognised him and so did he, when he addressed me in a half-baked Punjabi. *Sunoji tuada ki hal hae*, he said and added, "You are the same gentleman about whom I had made some nasty remarks at the bus stop about a year ago". I was dumbstruck and could only nod.

"I am really sorry for that day's behaviour. In fact I was upset on that day."

"But I didn't mind", I told him. "Rather I was somewhat amused."

"It was really nice of you", he continued in a tone that sounded apologetic. "But now my opinion about the Punjabis is altogether changed. I held them in high esteem."

"How come?" I was quick to ask him.

"Because of my daughter-in-law", he replied. "She is a Punjabi and a gem of a girl. The Punjabi 'kudi' has really transformed me. God bless her." There was glow on his face as he spoke.

59

BEG YOUR PARDON

At times, I wonder why we shoo away a beggar with a snarl "you seem to be in damn good health, why don't you do some work and earn?" But does anyone care? The beggar or the authorities who have made begging a cognisable offence?

He does not beg by choice. Probably, he has to, or he faces starvation. Borrow he can't for none will lend him anything, and steal he dare not—cops go sniffing everywhere. So the safest bet is beg for the *papi-pet.* Who knows, if given a choice, he may drop the begging-bowl.

But why single out a beggar? He is probably doing what he is 'destined' to do. What about others who are also begging in mere statement "I beg of you, please…", one very often hears, amounts to nothing but begging. And we beg even while praying to the Almighty.

What does a bureaucrat, a *babu* or for that matter who works to earn, do on the salary day? He only begs. Like a beggar who sits on a pavement or stands at a road crossing with a bowl, he extends his hand before the cashier. Similarly, a daily-wager is made to beg for his wages which rarely commensurate with the hard work he puts in all through the day.

What about businessman who stands before government officials, especially the income tax and sales tax, whenever he is cornered for his *hera-pheri.* He only begs. But none dares call him a beggar.

What does a politician do at the time of elections? He begs for votes. Like a beggar he considers the voters as his *Mai-Baap,* though it is a different matter that, once elected, the roles get reversed.

In the days bygone and probably there are many who might still be carrying the British legacy, whenever a junior addressed an application to his senior, he invariably used to begin with the words "I beg to state". Similarly, doesn't one 'beg' the other's pardon in the course of one's conversation?

While still on begging, I was somewhat surprised to read the other day that anti-social elements and local dons, who are hand-in-glove with local civic authorities and police, take 'commission' from the beggars, for allowing them to use a particular 'place' or 'point'. 'The hafta' differs from place to place, crossing to crossing and point to point. The maximum is charged from the beggars who are allowed to 'function' outside the temples and places of worship.

So when you see a beggar next time, be a little considerate, for we are all sailing in the same boat.

60

TODAY'S LULLABY

The four-month-old child was crying for about half-an-hour or so. Her mother's efforts to calm her down were proving futile. Even breast-feeding did not work.

Both the lady and her husband, who were hosting a party to celebrate their wedding anniversary, were really in a soup, so to say, and feeling somewhat embarrassed.

The pitch of the child's cries was so high that even the Pankaj Udhas ghazal, which the music system played, got drowned in them.

Some experienced ladies among the guests also offered to lend a helping hand to the harassed mother. Turn by turn they tried all the 'tricks' they had learnt through their own experience, but the child just refused to oblige them. In fact every renewed effort found the child in a more aggressive mood.

"Probably she is feeling uneasy in this suffocating place," came a suggestion from a guest. "Take her out in the open, she will certainly feel better." A young girl offered her services and took the child out in the lawn. But the cries continued. They were now accompanied by occasional hiccups also. The child was brought back and handed over to her mother.

The child's grandmother, who does baby-sitting while the child's parents are away on their jobs, was also surprised at the child's defiant mood. "She never behaves like this. She cries only when her feed time is around. Otherwise she just plays and sleeps all through the day."

"Put *heeng ka lep* on her tummy," suggested an old lady. "Probably she is having tummy-ache."

The *heeng* paste was prepared and applied on the child's tummy. Barring some momentary relief, the child was back to her old crying rhythm.

The child was again taken to the bedroom by her mother, who tried to put her to sleep by humming a lullaby. There was a sudden lull, not in the cries of the child, but in the mother's humming. The tired mother had probably started feeling drowsy herself.

The Pankaj Udhas cassette was over. "Let us have the 'choli' song and let the youngsters dance," said a lady whose teenage daughter was keen to perform a dance.

The *Khalnayak* CD was inserted in the music system and forwarded to play the 'choli' song. In order to have the 'desired' effect (or probably, to drown the child's cries), the volume was put on full blast.

But, lo' and behold, the moment the song came on the loudspeakers of the music system, the child stopped crying. The mother came out running to the drawing room and screamed with joy, "She has stopped crying." The child had a faint smile on her lips.

Surprisingly, the child didn't cry again. Rather, she went to sleep without making much fuss, as the 'choli' song was being played and replayed for the benefit of the young dancers.

61

A MATTER OF COMPANY

It is said that one is known by the company one keeps. But I hold the view that one has no choice in this matter. A person in whose company one is eager to move, may not find the latter's very likeable or desirable. Similarly, an individual whom one wants to keep at an arm's length may be riding on one's shoulders all the time.

Take the case of intellectuals who always prefer to move in the company of those who can match their wits. They may feel somewhat out of place amidst ordinary mortals, though they should know that the latter can benefit a lot from their company.

Similarly, those who are brilliant in studies always like to interact with those who can match their brilliance. In the company of duffers, they may be considered *Andhon mein kaana raja*, a description they would not like to be associated with.

I also hold the view that despite the peers and seers sermonising about equality irrespective of caste, creed, and gender, in reality it is not so. A rich person rarely wants to be in the company of poor, though the latter may consider himself very lucky and privileged in the company of the former. A *chandi ki deewar* is always there to prevent any interaction between the haves and have-nots.

But I think that without getting close to others one cannot know much about them. I have observed that even the most disliked person may prove to be a very lovable one, in case one gets a chance to move in his company. This, very often, happens at the workplace. A colleague, a senior or an assistant is simply shunned because his company is not considered desirable. But once one interacts with him or gets closer to him, one realises how wrong one was in his assessment.

But, perhaps, sycophants are the luckiest lot. They can adjust themselves to any and every company and go to any extent and never throw their hands up. The jibes and vibes have no effect on them. Rather, the more they are shunned, the more determined they get in their resolve to make renewed efforts to 'hit' their target. As a matter of fact, without the coveted company, their existence is just meaningless.

62

INDIA'S QUEUE CULTURE

I wonder why nobody has ever explored the possibility of exporting India's queue culture to foreign lands. We are quite rich in it, and the world at large can certainly benefit from it.

The queues have become an integral part of our lives and, probably the lifestyle too. We live queues, we breathe queues and we dream queues. And in case any day we will not find the queues at the places where they should have been, one can conclude that we are heading for some sort of catastrophe.

There are queues at the milk booths, public taps, places of public convenience, bus stops, post offices (even for buying postal stationery), booking and reservation centres at the railway stations and, of late, at cinema houses, fast food restaurants and other eating places, wine shops (despite our avid faith in prohibition), places of worship and, at times, at the cremation grounds.

We have queues of people outside the bungalows of ministers and other political leaders (the popularity of a minister or a leader is measured in terms of the length of the queue). The popularity of a religious leader is also known by the queues one sees outside his abode. By the same token, a medical practitioner is considered good only if there is a long queue at his clinic, though it hardly matters whether he is a qualified doctor or just a quack.

Some feel that standing in the queue is just a waste of time. But I beg to differ. The queues provide us an opportunity to be active and alert. I think if we are not standing in one queue or the other, we might be whiling our time by sleeping, gossiping and spreading rumours, fighting among ourselves or, may be, busy producing the future queue-makers.

There is yet another aspect of the queue culture, which only we Indians have perfected. It is the art of queue breaking and jumping. It is the real example of survival of the fittest. Only the rough and tough survive in the queues, the simple and timid remain stranded or are pushed aside.

However, there is no doubt that our queue culture is something we should be proud of and must explore the possibility of exporting it to other countries. To start with, a highly experienced (not the ministers and the VIPs because they have no experience of the queues) and high-powered delegation should be sent to different parts of the world to explore the possibility of establishing centres where glimpses of the Indian queue culture can be provided to the people elsewhere.

63

UNTAINTED BY POWER

When he was fit and fine the late Comrade Ram Kishan was a very regular visitor, especially on every Tuesday, to the Hanuman Temple located on Baba Kharak Singh Marg in New Delhi. Clad in spotless white khadi kurta-payjama and wearing a Gandhi cap, he would just take his shoes off, wash his hands and face, buy 'prasad' and without making any fuss walk to the fag-end of the queue, notwithstanding its length. Tall and lanky, he stood out in the crowd.

At times I wondered whether others in the queue or the people and police personnel around the temple were aware of the fact that the Comrade was once the Chief Minister of Punjab, and that too before it got bifurcated into three separate identities. Had it been so they would have certainly exchanged pleasantries with him or at least asked him to 'ignore' the queue.

Once inside the temple, he would look around and bend his head time and again in reverence, taking the Lord's name. Like any other worshipper he was jostled and pushed around, without anybody caring for his age or the position he had once held. He never complained and always had a smile on his face.

"Why don't you disclose your identity to them?" I had once asked him.

"Why should I do that?" he counter-queried.

"You would not be required to stand in the queue and a priest would take you to the side door for *darshan*", I said.

"What is so special about me"? he was quick to observe and added, "I am like any other visitor to the temple." I was touched by his humbleness.

"You are so regular to the temple. At least I find you here on every Tuesday. What do you ask from the God?" I asked him one day out of curiosity.

He paused for a moment and replied, "I pray for my country's prosperity and peace in the world and above all seek the Almighty's forgiveness for any wrong I might have done to any person, unknowingly."

The other regular visitor to the temple on Tuesdays was Sajjan Kumar, the former member of Parliament from outer Delhi. His arrival used to put on alert the police personnel on duty who would immediately ensure that this high-profile MP was not put to any inconvenience and also spent 'minimum' time in the temple.

Headed and followed by the black cats, he just would not bother to look at the queue, leave alone standing in it and taking his turn. The priests also would give him VIP treatment. He was ushered in from the door which is used by others for exit.

It was probably a coincidence that one of the Tuesdays, when Comrade Ram Kishan was standing in the queue just ahead of me, Sajjan Kumar also came to the temple. He almost passed by the side where the Comrade stood, but did not care to look at him.

"Does he not recognise you?" I asked the Comrade.

"I have no idea," he replied with his usual disarming manner and smilingly added, "I am only a *Sevak*, but he is a *Neta*."

"The times have really changed." I had mused to myself.

64

THE MIDDLE NAME

The trend of christening a newly-born without a middle name probably started somewhere in the fifties. Till then, no name was considered 'complete' or 'full' unless it had a middle name and it really required quite on effort to find an appropriate one. The criterion used was to have a middle name which should rhyme well with the first name, though for all practical purposes it had only an ornamental or 'cosmetic' value and nothing else.

Unlike western and southern India where age-old practice is to have a father's or the native place's name as a middle name, in northern India there used to be a set of 'names' from which the selection was made. Some of them which invariably found place in case of boys were 'Pal', 'Kumar', 'Nath', 'Das', 'Rai', 'Lal', 'Raj' etc., depending, of course, on what rhymed with the first name. For example, only Prakash could go well with 'Om' or 'Das' with 'Lakshman'.

Surprisingly, my grandfather altogether deviated from the set pattern and chose (probably after working out some astrological permutations and combinations as he was a great believer in horoscopes) 'Swaroop', 'Bandhu', 'Bhanu' and 'Rattan' as middle names for his sons, who again 'reverted to the commonly-used middle names when their turn came to christen their progeny.

Unlike the male child where the choice was quite wide, the selection was limited to only 'Kumari', 'Rani' or 'Devi' in case of the girls. Here again, the choice was confined to 'Kumari' (meaning an unwed girl) in most of the cases, which automatically got dropped after a girl was married.

What started as trend became fashion with some in the later years. Finding their middle names of no particular significance many decided to drop them and 'fell in line', as the cliche goes. But to their dismay, they were neither here nor there. But what I consider to be a unique case was that of film-maker and cine-star Raj Kapoor who opted for the middle name and decided to drop the first. His full name was 'Tilak Raj Kapoor.'

But I think these middle names have boosted the ego of those who believe in caste system and is, certainly, a setback for those who have faith in the caste-less society. These days names, without fail, have surnames with the result that the castes have got more pronounced.

However, I still believe that middle name has its own charm, and there is no harm in giving it a place of pride where it fits in well. It probably, all depends on the parents to be, who, finding something amiss in their names, may return to this old practice of having a middle name while christening their siblings. Well, good luck!

65

CRIMINALS AND ELECTIONS

The more I hear about the decriminalisation of politics, the more I get the feeling that my chances of either becoming a Member of Parliament or of an Assembly are getting brighter. Almost every political party has declared that in no case will a person with a criminal record be given the party ticket in the elections. This has encouraged me further.

But the question is: how will the political parties come to know whether a person has a criminal record or not? Afterall, no individual will admit of his own that he is a criminal or has a criminal record. Moreover, who will sit in judgement on such a delicate and probably provocative matter.

Will the political parties ask the police stations to check their records and provide them with a list of those persons who might have been involved in criminal activities at one time or the other? But there is every possibility that the police, fearing the wrath of criminals, might only give the list of honest and upright persons and ignore altogether the criminals. The police may even hold secret talks or consultations with the criminals before submitting the list. In such a situation, only the criminals are likely to get the ticket from political parties.

Maybe the political parties will hire the services of a computer firm or a consultancy agency and ask it to design a "questionnaire" which the prospective candidates will be required to fill in. The filled-in forms might be fed to the computers to check the credentials of the candidates. But I am sure the criminals might even play havoc with the computers and come out unscathed.

The political organisations might even hire the services of detective agencies to probe the past of the prospective candidates. But here again the hardcore criminals might escape the eye of a detective. Similarly, the use of a "lie-detector" to ascertain whether a prospective candidate is telling the truth or trying to hide something about his criminal background may not prove very effective.

There is every likelihood that the parties may ask the candidates to attach with their applications an "oath" duly attested by an Oath Commissioner, saying that "to the best of their knowledge and understanding, they have never indulged in any criminal activity", and haul them up in case it becomes known that they are "criminals". But the question is who will dare initiate action against them once they become the "honourable" members of legislative bodies?

I have another fear. With the political parties getting firm on not giving the ticket to the persons with a criminal record, it may not be possible to find the required number of candidates for the elections. In that case they may not be left with any option but to fall back upon the criminals.

Though the chances of my getting the ticket from any party to fight the elections are somewhat bright, I doubt that the politicians with a criminal record and their henchmen will ever allow the political organisations to give the ticket to those having clean image. They may liquidate such candidates before these people even file their nomination papers, rig the elections or get themselves elected unopposed.

66

A CASE OF POETIC INJUSTICE

I had not expected to meet Gopal again. But when I did after a decade or so, and that too in a police station, where I had gone in connection with the renewal of my passport, I just couldn't believe my eyes. He was being roughed up by an ASI who was trying to extract a confession from him. He was accused of stealing some items from a grocery shop.

Seeing me, Gopal picked up some courage to plead, "I am not a thief. I have not stolen anything from that shop." Pointing towards me, he said, "Ask him if you don't believe me. He knows me very well."

I was quick to react. "Yes, Inspector, I know him. I don't think he would have indulged in this sort of a thing." However, with days of stubble on his face, dishevelled hair, crumpled kurta and faded jeans and a dirty cotton bag hanging from his shoulder, anybody could have entertained doubts about him.

"But he is refusing to show his bag," the ASI said. "Probably he is carrying the booty in it."

Gopal was one of my assistants in the office and had resigned his job to try his luck as a song-writer in Bollywood. All the five years or so he worked with me, I always found him scribbling some *nazams* and *ghazals* in Urdu, and very often gave me for reading. I really found them of quality and a high standard.

"I want to be a song-writer," he used to tell me. He sent his *ghazals* and *geets* to some prominent film-makers and music directors. There was never any response from them. But when he found that one of the song-writers of repute had used his work in one of the films, he was shocked and had even protested; but to no avail.

On my suggestion he started sending his *ghazals* to some Urdu newspapers and magazines for publication. Though they were used as 'fillers', he never got any payment. But he was happy to see his poetry in print and proudly told everybody about it. However, his dream to finally land up in the filmdom and be a Shailendra, a Shakeel Badayuni, a Sahir Ludhianwi, or a Neeraj, remained unfulfilled.

"Forget about it and concentrate on your job," I had been advising him. "I am sure luck will favour you one day."

But then one day in a mood of desperation he resigned his job and decided to go to Bombay. The fact that his sister had got a job and was engaged to one of her colleagues, prompted him to take this hasty step.

"Please ask him to show his bag," the ASI asked me "Why don't you show your bag?" I pleaded with Gopal.

He reluctantly removed the bag from his shoulder and handed it over to me. In a reflex action, I just poured the contents of the bag on the ASI's table.

There were three or four diaries, some scraps of paper, and letters of introduction and recommendation addressed to some film-makers and music directors. The diary and the scraps of paper contained his *ghazals* and *nazams.*

"Didn't I tell you that I am not a thief?" Gopal asked the ASI in an aggressive tone. I was relieved of the tension. The ASI let him go without any further fuss.

Despite my insisting on him to come to my house, he refused. "I will go to my sister's house and stay with her for a few days and then go back to Bombay to try my luck again. After all Rajinder Krishan succeeded only after making repeated efforts," he said, as we parted.

This happened a year back. I am yet to come across a film where credit titles carry his name as a song-writer. Maybe one day I will.

67

EXPORTING SCAMS

I wonder why nobody so far has thought of exporting scams. With one scam or the other surfacing now and then, we have acquired a good deal of expertise to teach the world about the techniques involved in exceeding the scams of any and every type. In fact, we can be pioneers in this field.

A good number of Indians, specially the politicians and the bureaucrats, have now sufficient knowledge to explain the intricacies of executing the scams without anybody coming to know about them and extricating from them without any scar.

Similarly, we have also mastered the art of using the scams for political purposes, specially to demolish the political opponents, something about which the politicians all over the world will be too keen to know. At the same time, those politicians who get involved in the scams have also learnt the techniques of getting the maximum "political" mileage from the scams, thus balancing the scales and giving benefit to none.

We have now a good number of sleuths who have acquired an indepth knowledge of investigating the scams, and manipulating them as and when they are asked to do so, something very unique for the world to learn. Similarly, we now have very knowledgeable officers in the judiciary who can impart training to the judicial officers of any part of the world about the trial and possible prosecution of the scam accused.

The main plus point, which should help us in popularising the Indian scams in the foreign lands, is the non-involvement of the fair sex. Any scam sans sex is less harmful and less dangerous than the one that involves a member of the fair sex. This point has to be highlighted while exploring the foreign markets. The countries which have become notorious for sex scandals will be too glad to opt for the Indian scams.

Another added advantage of the Indian scams is that it has a "code" language which can be deciphered only by its writer and can be interpreted by him only.

As I foresee a demand for social "diaries" (which do not wear and tear for decades) and "pens" (which do not smudge the paper), we must issue licences for their manufacture immediately.

We can establish an Indian Institute for Scam Studies both for Indian and foreign students. However, preference should be given to the foreign students who are ready to pay their fees in dollars, enabling the country to earn the foreign exchange, always in short supply. But there should be no "hawala" dealings.

Like the institute, we can also set up an Export Council for Scams to propagate abroad the salient features of the Indian scams and explore the potential markets for their exports. Let the institute and the council be headed by those who were, and, are, involved in one scam or the other. But the big question is: who will bell the cat and how? Or somebody may say that the export suggestion itself has the contours of a scam.

68

NAME DROPPER PAR EXCELLENCE

I had heard about his name-dropping traits but had the first-hand experience only when he was transferred to my section. Fearing 'disruption' in the work. I had prepared myself for all the eventualities. But to my utter surprise he turned out to be an asset and not a liability for a decade or so he was in my section. Despite his being very busy with his 'social work' (that was how he used to describe his name-dropping game), he was not only uptodate with his own work but also used to go out of his way to help others in their work. In fact, by and by I had started enjoying and admiring him for his name-dropping game.

One had just to name a VIP, a minister or a high-up, and Mr ND (that was how I used to address him) would have many tales to tell about his acquaintance with him or her. To impress others he would always refer to them by their first names.

Mr ND was always surrounded by people who either sought his 'advice' or beseeched him to 'speak' to some minister or some high official on their behalf. He had never said no to anybody. He would promptly dial a number (most probably a non-existent one) and start talking with authority, invariably dropping names of some political heavy weights and some VVIPs thus giving an impression of how 'well-connected' or how 'close' he was with the powers-that-be or the persons-that-matter.

Mr ND always had some ready-made replies for the satisfaction of all those who came to seek his 'help' or 'assistance'. "I will talk to the minister concerned and let you know what he has to say," he would tell them. "I am attending a dinner tonight at Rashtrapati Bhavan alongwith the minister and will certainly take up the matter with him," he would say and also name some ministers and VIPs who might also be present at the dinner. Another stock reply he had for some was: "I am sorry, you have chosen a very wrong time. As the parliament is in session neither the minister nor his staff is free. But don't you worry. I am accompanying the minister on his tour this weekend and will certainly take up your case."

Alongwith his name-dropping game, Mr ND had also perfected the art of playing truant whenever he found himself 'cornered' or in 'hot waters'. He would simply vanish from the scene not for a day or two but weeks. Moreover, he would have some interesting, and probably cooked-up tales to tell on his return.

"You see I was aksed by the party High Command to go to Lucknow to meet the dissidents," he would say to create confidence among his 'seekers'. "I was sent to Bombay by the PM with an urgent message for the CM," was yet another stock reply for those who were keen to know about the reasons behind his sudden disappearance. One just couldn't dispute his statements because soon the places Mr ND supposed to have visited would witness some political developments or upheavals. Probably his intuition and understanding of political matters used to come to his aid.

However, it must be said to his credit that like other power-brokers and name-droppers he never indulged in his game of name-dropping for any considerations, cash or kind. It was probably the 'kick' he got because of the extra-attention he used to receive and the self-esteem he earned in the process made him play his name-dropping games.

The latest about Mr ND is that he is still very much in the game but has changed (naturally), his political loyalities.

69

CLINICALLY DOCTORED MATRIMONIALS

The horoscopes or *janam kundalis* have always played a role in matrimonial matters in our country. Many a time the negotiations just break because the horoscopes of the boy and girl do not conform or match. Those who think that the matching of the horoscopes are things of the past or is something in which only orthodox or backward looking parents or families believe in, are mistaken. The horoscopes and their matching continue to form a part of the negotiations and even educated and progressive persons do consult *pandits* and go by their advice.

It is, however, a different matter that despite all this matching and tallying of the horoscopes, there is no guarantee that the spouses would lead a trouble-free, smooth and harmonious marital life. They might, perhaps always be quarreling or remain on collision course, at times even resulting in separation and divorce.

A computer shop owner, who is doing roaring business in preparing computer *kundalis* and matching them for matrimonial purposes, says that the trend of matching the horoscopes of the boys and girls, is certainly catching up. He gets about a dozen clients everyday who come to him for matching horoscopes obviously meant for matrimonial purposes. Similarly, a *panditji*, who has a very large clientele, informs me that at least half a dozen parents approach him daily for tallying the horoscopes of prospective brides and grooms.

To a question whether they can find out from the horoscopes physical deformities, genetic defects and ailments like diabetes, etc. both the computer shop owner and the *panditji* replied in the negative. As such they said that they could forecast about some 'trouble' or 'mishap' that the would-be couples might face but nothing beyond that.

This brings us to the point that in addition to the matching of *girahs, ghars, avguns* and *guns*, the boys and girls should be asked to undergo medical check-ups and files prepared and exchanged between the families and cross-checked by some neutral medical experts.

The medical reports should contain details regarding blood groups, conditions of hypertension, diabetes, clinical reports of urine and blood tests, X-rays or ultra-sounds reports to detect tuberculosis, asthama or any venereal disease and now AIDS. The check-ups can cover all possible tests that can rule out any possibility of clinical or medical incompatibility between the boys and girls after marriage. All this will certainly help the couples in leading healthy marital lives and grow healthy families.

But these clinical reports will serve their purpose only if neither the parents nor the to be brides and grooms hide anything from the doctors or play foul.

70

A CLASS BY THEMSELVES

Although I reside in a colony which is very much a part of South Delhi parliamentary constituency, yet I have no right to call myself a South Delhiite. Probably the so-called genuine South Delhiites may even haul me up if I dare to do so. Only those who have their residences (minus of course who are occupying the government accommodation) beyond Dhaula Kuan, and specially on both sides of Mahatma Gandhi Road (nee Ring Road) between Dhaula Kuan and Maharani Bagh have the right to call themselves South Delhiites.

But then what is so special about South Delhiites? Are they in any way different from those residing in North, West and East Delhi? Why do they think they are a class apart from the other Delhiite? To me a South Delhiite is like any other Delhiite be he or she is a resident of a Katra of Chandni Chowk or a group housing society beyond the Yamuna. I am sure the IQ of a South Delhiite is no way better than a person residing in Rohini in West Delhi.

Like any other area of Delhi, the colonies which constitute South Delhi, also have their quota of slums, Lal Dora villages, open garbage dumps, stinking lanes and bylanes, power shutdowns, water scarcity, etc. I am sure that in regard to air or noise pollution also South Delhi will be as good or worse as any other areas of Delhi.

The South Delhiites claim that some of the best and modern shopping complexes are located in their area only. But then household name so far as shopping is concerned continues to be the Ajmal Khan Road and I am sure majority of South Delhiites must be doing their shopping from there only.

I am told that the intellectuals and men of letters, those who call themselves intelligentsia, prefer to stay in South Delhi. Well, if they find the jungle of concrete, devoid of greenery a better place it is their prerogative. But I am sure if they just look beyond South Delhi, they will find that there are many other areas in North, West and East Delhi which are also best suited for their literary pursuits and may provide them better food for thought.

We are told that the rich and business class too have preference for South Delhi. However, if somebody is to conduct a survey, it may turn out to be a shocking revelation for many South Delhiites that some of the top businessmen (probably they are yet to learn from their counterparts in South Delhi the art of vulgar display of their wealth) reside in North and East Delhi. Incidentally I may be excused for my impertinence if I say that the South Delhiites lack in aesthetic sense so far as the architecture is concerned. Probably the same holds good for interior designing also.

But the fact remains that a South Delhiite does carry an air of superiority vis-a-vis other Delhiites. Had it not been so, the matrimonial ads would not be mentioning this fact so boldly and proudly. But my contention is how a boy or a girl residing in South Delhi is different from the one who had no choice in selecting his or her residence. The fault probably lies with parents who chose to live in colonies which didn't carry the stamp of South Delhi. Do the boys and girls of South Delhi make better life partners? Well, I have my own doubts. But how about a boy residing in South Extn. falling in love with a girl living in an LIG flat in Vikaspuri and finally marrying her? The hapless status-conscious parents can only fret and fume.

But the other day when in confused frame of mind, I asked a friend, who resides in South Delhi: "What is so special about South Delhi?", he promptly replied, "The land prices. A square yard of land costs two lakh rupees."

"But one needs only ten by six feet space finally and that too without paying for it and sharing with many others," I said somewhat philosophically.

"You will not understand all this," my friend retorted. "Only a South Delhiite can feel the kick of being a South Delhiite."

Well, I am still not able to figure it out.

71

BUMPY STAR TRACKS

Frankly speaking I do believe in astrology, palmistry, numerology, etc. and all that is associated with these sciences, if you would like to call them so. I have been going to the practitioners of these professions, and also to soothsayers, to seek their guidance whenever I found myself in some 'trouble' or got 'encircled' by some 'adverse' circumstances. But, to my dismay, I always found myself in more confused frame of mind after consulting them. In fact I used to feel more dejected and demoralized after visiting them.

I have very often observed that the *Pandits* of these professions invariably confuse their clients. They create a fear-psychosis in them. They couch their language in so many 'ifs' and 'buts' that one suddenly finds oneself in 'take it' or 'leave it' situation. In case one refuses to follow the 'remedies' suggested by them and something 'adverse' happens, they blame it on you and 'honee' (something destined to happen). And if everything goes smooth and works out 'well' for you, they take all the credit.

Similarly in the matrimonial matters also the matching of the horoscopes has now become inseparable part of the negotiations. But does everything goes well with the couples whose horoscopes are matched and everything found 'excellent'? At least I have my own doubts. I know of a friend who had bribed a *Pandit* to match his daughter's horoscope (it was manipulated, my friend once confessed to me) with that of a boy who otherwise was a fit match for his daughter. Even after two decades or so everything has worked out well in their marital life. But on the other hand, my eldest sister whose horoscope was matched by not one but three *Pandits*, continued to lead a miserable life, because her husband deserted her within five years of the marriage. It all sounds paradoxical. Isn't it?

I also religiously go through weekly 'forecasts' carried by most of the newspapers. But again I find myself in utter confusion after going through these columns. Rarely they have similar or common things to say. Rather they contradict each other. Moreover, these forecasts rarely come close to the 'happenings of the week'. The contributors of these columns claim that these forecasts are only 'general' in nature and not very specific from an individual's point of view. Well, then they are of no consequence for an individual. Or may be if one doesn't follow the 'tips' contained in these forecasts, one can find oneself in still a worse situation. Well, I am at my wits' end and find myself somewhat in a Shakesperian situation: To believe or not to believe.

72

WAIT FOR THE 'JAIMALA'

The Groom's father, a retired Major, was firm on maintaining punctuality about the marriage ceremonies and also wanted the bride's side to stick to the schedule.

But no one took Major Sahib seriously. "It is just not possible to maintain punctuality in marriages", he was told. But he stuck to his guns, so to say, and ensured that the 'baraat' reached the 'assembly point' as per the time indicated in the invitation card.

A messenger was sent to the bride's place to inform that the marriage party would be reaching there in about ten minutes! But the message came back that as the bride had not come back from the beauty parlour the baraat's departure might be delayed by about half-an-hour or so.

"Nothing doing", roared Major Sahib, and asked the marriage party to proceed. Even some youngsters and groom's friends who were eager to perform 'bhangara' were snubbed and told to obey the 'marching orders'.

The marriage party reached the bride's place right at eight, the schedule time of its arrival. All-round there was confusion. The bride was still at the beauty parlour. Frantic calls were made and messengers sent to the beauty parlour to bring back the bride. But she was only half-way through with her bridal make-up exercise. As there was no electricity, everything was taking extra time.

The time ticked by. The dinner was coming to an end and the guests had already started dispersing. The groom anxiously waited for the bride to proceed with 'jaimala' and other ceremonies. Helpless, Major Sahib sat in a corner with a sullen face and 'lectured' about maintaining punctuality to all those who were prepared to lend their ears to him.

The bride was back only at ten-thirty. Everybody had a sigh of relief. But what shocked them was the awful make-up (probably done in the candle light) the bride had so much so that the video-cameraman had to request her time and again to clean her face to remove extra layers of powder and other beauty aids.

"I didn't know that the bridal make-up these days forms an important part of the marriage ceremonies," Major Sahib was heard saying as the bride and groom got ready to perform the 'jaimala' ceremony. However, there were not many to grace the occasion.

73

FUNCTION(AL) PROBLEMS

The minister had not been in the news for quite some time. But as the elections were round the corner, he was desperate to get some publicity.

Though he had been invariably making his presence felt by greeting the people of his constituency on Diwali, Holi, Eid, Pongal (to please Tamilians who constitute at least 3 per cent of the electorate in his constituency), Baisakhi, Dussehra and for that matter even New Year, he was not sure whether the people of his constituency would vote for him.

He had also been without fail attending marriage and mundan ceremonies and jagrans in case that brought him in the public eye. At times he even made himself available for the opening ceremonies and laying of foundation stones of some obscure shopping complex or a place of public convenience. In fact, he was always out to grab any opportunity that gave him some political mileage.

But the urgency to get publicity arose because of the elections.

The minister called a meeting of his supporters and party workers and asked them to do something to get some publicity before the election code became operative. After a long discussion a supporter suggested that the best for the minister would be to inaugurate the work of filling up of the *barsaati-nala* (rain drain) that ran through the major part of his constituency. Moreover, it had been a crying demand of the people of his constituency. The minister was quick to jump at the suggestion and gave his green signal.

Post-haste arrangements were made to organise the function. Multi-coloured posters, with the minister's picture displayed prominently, were printed and pasted all over the area. Even the hoardings were put up at all the vantage points. Invitations were sent to media persons and some VIPs of the area. Tea and light refreshments were promised after the ceremony.

The exercise of inviting tenders and assigning the job to a contractor was undertaken with such a speed that, what otherwise might have taken months or years, was completed in a week's time. All the hurdles that could have come in the way of holding of the ceremony were cleared at the highest level.

The D-day came. Hardly 40 persons, including about a dozen workers of the contractor, had assembled by 10 a.m., the scheduled time of the ceremony. No media person was there to cover the event.

Some singers were arranged and asked to sing film songs to keep the assembly busy and, if possible, to attract more crowd. But nothing worked. The *shamiana* continued to look deserted.

Time and again the minister was asked to delay his arrival. But when he finally did come the crowd had further thinned. The minister was furious. He blamed the organisers for putting up such a poor show. But there was no other go for him.

As the minister broke a coconut and was in the process of throwing some sand with shovel with hardly audible clappings from the crowd surrounding him, a thunderous applause was heard from the adjoining shopping complex. Thousands of people had gathered there to have a glimpse of a cine star who had come to inaugurate a beauty parlour. There were dozens of video and still photography cameramen to cover the function.

Needless to say the minister lost the election and with his exit the work on the drain came to a standstill.

74

IN AN AGE OF WALKS

This is an age of walks. At least I feel so and can cite many examples to prove my point.

The medical fraternity have realised that only medication cannot help a patient. It must be supplemented by walk. Whether one is suffering from a cardiac problem or obesity, the doctor is sure to prescribe "walks" preferably brisk, both in the morning and evening. "The walks will do a lot of good to you," the doctor advises.

Then we have "walk-outs". At any gathering where one finds oneself isolated, or not getting attention, feeling bored because somebody is playing on the nerves, "walking out" is the best way to attract everybody's attention. And if one says something "nasty" while "walking out", one cannot escape others' attention.

The parliamentarians and members of the legislative assemblies in India have found through experience that the only way to get public and Press attention is to stage a "walk-out". They know now that even the well-said points or issues raised during the debates and discussions do not get them the desired publicity as the "walk-outs". However, the "walk-out" is certainly be a very costly affair.

If there are "walk-outs", there have to be "walk-ins" also. It is logical. That is why probably, of late, there are more "walk-in" interviews. The traditional and well-tested way of inviting applications, holding interviews, and then selecting the right person has already been dispensed with. This not only puts to loss the postal authorities but at times the railways also.

To me, however, these "walk-in" interviews mean depriving some best and well-qualified persons from being selected for a post for which they are well-suited. An outstation candidate or the one putting up quite at a distance from the place of interview, howsoever capable he or she (a lady feels further handicapped) might be, will not be able to make it to a "walk-in" interview. A local candidate is certainly in an advantageous position.

Like "walk-ins", the "walk-offs", are also of a recent origin. They have, in fact, become part and parcel of different games, be it cricket, hockey or tennis. At times "walk-offs" are staged on very flimsy grounds or when the defeats are imminent, or to give some rest to the players. Maybe we might hear soon somebody saying that he got "walk-off fixed".

The "cat-walks" are something very unique. Though smartly dressed damsels walk on the ramps with their difficult-to-decipher body language at display, there are no "cats" around to give them company.

Though "cat-walks" are at least a pleasing-to-eye affair, the "fire-walks", undertaken by those seeking heavenly blessings or doing by way of penance, on the other hand, create a feeling of fear in many.

Well, won't you agree with me that this is an age of walks. I think you do.

75

WITH NO REGRETS

When I decided to quit a well-secured government job within a year of joining it, many were taken by surprise. However, I was certain that had I continued in the job for another year or so, I would have got "rusted" to the extent that ultimately I would have become a good-for-nothing-fellow, a tag I would have carried till the time of my superannuation. There was no job satisfaction.

Despite my repeated requests to my seniors to give me some "work", I was not assigned any duty for about three months or so. My eagerness to get myself involved in some "gainful" work brought only derisive remarks from my colleagues, especially those who were in the habit of gossiping, enjoying extended tea and lunch sessions, playing cards and, of course, keeping the bosses in "good humour".

I practically cooled my heels for about three months without doing any work. However, even when finally I was assigned the work, it brought no joy.

Though appointed on a technical job, the work I was asked to do could have been done even by a daftry. "Please link all the relevant files", my boss had told me. About three dozen files were handed over to me. I was busy for about a month trying to "link" the files but did not come across a single file which could be "linked" to another. "Doesn't matter", the boss said when I reported back to him. "You will be given some other assignment".

The boss started routing all the files through me and instructed the staff also to do the same. The idea was probably to keep me busy. But the whole exercise turned out to be totally "unrewarding". The job required no "brain" or "labour". Barring the putting of flags like "DFA" (draft for approval), "PUC" (paper under consideration) and of some assorted alphabets (for example, the letter received from the party is placed at Flag "A"), I did nothing. It used to take me about 20 minutes to handle about two dozen files. For the rest of the day I had no work.

But what irked me the most was the snail's speed at which the files used to move and that too without taking any decision on the matters, at times, even very urgent.

I was getting frustrated. There were two options open to me: either to become a part of the "system" or resign. I decided to quit. However, I have no regrets for taking that momentous decision. The "system" was so deeply stuck in the grooves (and I think it continues to be so even today). I couldn't have adjusted myself to it.

76

GANDHI WHO?

Have you read any of the works of Gandhi? I asked my nephew the other day. "Gandhi who?" he counterquestioned me. I had not used, rather deliberately, the prefix 'Mahatma' and suffix 'Ji'.

I was shocked. "How many Gandhis did our country have?" I queried.

"Why we had Indira, Rajiv and Sanjay," he said. "And now we have Sonia, Priyanka, Rahul, Varun and Menaka." He probably did not know about Feroze Gandhi, Indira's husband, otherwise he would have added his name too.

"The Gandhi I am talking about is 'Mahatma Gandhi', the Father of the Nation," I explained.

"Oh, you are talking about Gandhi', whose *samadhi* we have on the banks of Yamuna," my nephew said. "I had once gone to his *samadhi* with one of my friends. The grass there is beautiful. But the tragedy is they do not allow people to have picnics there."

I was again shocked. It is no use talking further to him about Mahatma Gandhi, I said to myself, and left it at that.

But why blame the young soul? Someone hooked on Mills and Boon books, and born in the mid-seventies, he can be excused for not having known much about Mahatma Gandhi beyond his *samadhi*. Probably nobody made any serious effort to introduce Gandhian literature to him.

But then what can one say about a gentleman, who holds a very senior position in the central government, when asked whether he had read any of the 'works' of Mahatma Gandhi, replied, "I don't think Mahatma Gandhi wrote any book."

"No my dear, he has many books to his credit," I informed him.

"Oh, is that so", he exclaimed. "I thought he had only held prayer meetings and preached *satyagraha* and non-violence, and told people to offer your right cheek in the event of somebody slapping your left cheek."

I pitied the gentleman for his ignorance. But, unlike my nephew, he didn't talk about the other 'Gandhis'. At least he claimed that he had liked the film 'Gandhi' and had seen it half-a-dozen times. "It is a wonderful movie but lacks the dramatic touch that good Indian movies should have."

"For your information, even through his talks, Mahatma Gandhi had almost touched upon each and every aspect of our social, economic and political life," I told the gentleman by way of information. "Not only that, he had solutions to all our problems. I wish you could visit some good library and go through some of the anthologies of Gandhian literature."

The gentleman did not take serious note of my suggestion. "And dirty my hands by handling books buried under all that dust?" he shot back. "I don't think his thoughts have any relevance now."

I was dumbfounded, not knowing whether to pursue the matter or simply surrender. I chose the second option.

But then another frightening thought crossed my mind. The gentleman is probably not the only Indian holding such an opinion. There might be lakhs and crores like him in the country.

77

RIGHT MESSAGE GOES HOME

We had not comprehended that our new boss would turn out to be a very difficult person to deal with. Without giving the staff an opportunity to "understand" or "know" him well, he started showing his colours, so to say, right from day one itself.

Being a product of a foreign university and having served some of the prestigious organisations abroad, he wanted to "restructure" the office on the pattern of the establishments he was associated with and was keen to introduce "new work culture" among the staff.

The staff had no quarrel with the boss's plans and was willing to give a fair trial to them. But what upset the staff was the boss's uneven moods, nasty utterances, bouts of anger and tantrums. Everyday there were new tensions, so much so that a stage had reached where things were getting beyond everybody's endurance.

We had two options: either to submit meekly to the boss's whims and fancies or make an effort to "tame" him. The majority favoured the latter.

As different proposals were being debated upon, I had casually suggested that we should "tackle" the boss through his wife. There was no logic behind my suggestion, but still everybody fell for it.

After days of deliberations, it was decided that a cultural evening be organised and the boss's wife should be asked to be the chief guest. Half the battle was won when the lady accepted our invitation without giving even a second thought.

The lady arrived for the show quite early. She moved freely among the staff and their family members exchanged pleasantries with them. The boss only shadowed her.

As the programme of songs, skits, dances, etc. progressed, two ladies from among the staff were asked to keep constant company with the chief guest. The idea was to pay extra attention to her.

The climax of the cultural evening was a specially written skit portraying the character of a new boss who wanted to "restructure" the office with "impractical" plans. The boss was furious but his wife enjoyed every bit of the skit.

The boss was again furious, when while proposing a vote of thanks, the chief guest was praised for her pleasing personality and cheerful disposition. The lady, however, was really delighted.

The staff had expected that the boss would be in a very nasty mood the next day, and feared that he might take disciplinary action against some. But to everybody's surprise he was exceptionally in a very cheerful mood. We were further surprised when through a circular he thanked the staff for organising such a "lively" evening and expressed the hope that in future also there would be more of such functions because these "help in creating better understanding among the staff, in particular the seniors and juniors." It seemed the "message" had gone home well. Even I had not thought that a suggestion made in a very casual manner would work.

78

BEWARE OF THE SLEIGHT OF HAND

Kabariwalas, mechanics, whether of automobiles or electronics goods and so-called skilled workers (we rarely see their certificates before requisitioning their services) like plumbers, electricians and carpenters, are a strange lot. At least I feel so.

They invariably indulge in one upmanship (thank God there are no ladies in these businesses) games to impress you, though finally turn out to be the chips of the same block.

It is an acknowledged fact that *Kabariwala,* without an exception, indulges in all sorts of malpractices to cheat and hoodwink you. But still the man you are dealing with will claim that he is the only one in his trade who is honest and the rest are just cheats. He even volunteers to give you some clues about the *hera-pheri* his co-professionals indulge in.

But I am certain that as he talks to you he may be trying to play the same tricks with you.

The mechanics, on the other hand, invariably lecture you about their expertise and in the process will not hesitate to say all sorts of bad things about the novices in their profession who do not know their job well.

Even if you tell them that there are some efficient people around, who are equally good, if not better, they continue parroting about their own expertise and proficiency.

But my experience is that the mechanics who talk more rarely do good jobs but are masters in preparing hefty bills.

The plumbers, electricians and carpenters are yet another lot who indulge in the game of one-upmanship to win over your confidence. They invariably tell you that those who have been attending to your jobs were cheats.

But to your horror you may soon realise that the gentlemen, who claimed to be very honest and expert, and fiddled with your gadgets and wares to an extent that you are left with no option to replace them.

But can we escape from these wheeler-dealers? The answer is probably 'no' only. We need them.

But then I have an advice to offer. Don't stick to one fellow.

Give him an occasional shock to make him realise that there are many around who are equally good at the game of one-upmanship and can handle the job better.

79

AGAINST EFFIGIES

Burning an effigy is a ritual without which no agitation or protest is considered complete these days. It is performed either to register protest against an individual or to highlight an issue or a problem agitating the minds of the people at large.

But I have my own doubts about this effigy burning business. Take the case of burning an effigy of an individual. I don't think the individual is affected at all by the "heat" generated as his effigy is being set aflame.

Rather he might feel elated that he has been considered worthy of this honour. If clever enough (for instance no politician will miss this chance), he might even cash in on this opportunity and draw maximum mileage from his burnt effigy.

Similarly burning of an effigy to convey concern or to highlight an issue or a problem carry no meaning unless the flames of the burnt effigy are able to achieve the "desired" results.

I have no idea who makes these effigies. Most of the time it looks as if some amateurs have done a hurried job with rags and paper put together. Such poor workmanship does no credit either to the effigy burners or the one whose effigy is being burnt.

It would be best to assign the job of effigy-making to the craftsmen who make effigies of Ravana, Kumbhakarna and Meghnad for the Dussehra celebrations.

This will also provide round-the-year jobs to these seasonal workers. But what pains me the most is that at times the effigies are just "namesake" or "symbolic" and bear no resemblance to the person whom it is meant to represent. It is really an insult to the person whose effigy is being burnt and a very shabby and disgraceful way of highlighting an issue or a problem. We must have more attractive and well-done effigies. This will attract more audiences.

The other lacuna found in these effigy-burning shows is that very rarely do celebrities or VIPs participate in them. That would attract more media attention.

I have a suggestion to make to these effigy-burning enthusiasts. Confine your protests to the winter months only. At least all those who take the trouble of burning an effigy will get some warmth.

Effigy burning might be considered a bizarre way of protesting. But then, it has become a universally accepted practice.

80

BRIDE-SHOPPING!

When despite advertising in the matrimonial columns of almost all the national dailies coupled with the efforts made by relations and friends, one of my foreign-born-and-bred nephews, couldn't find a suitable match for himself, I really felt sorry for him.

The girls he met outsmarted and outwitted him in their face-to-face and one-to-one meetings arranged on specific requests of the girls' parents. "We will come into the picture only when the girls give us the go-ahead signal," was the general refrain of the parents.

The incident reminded me of the times when the parents used to take all the decisions right from 'finding' and 'selecting' a boy or a girl and holding negotiations with the parents. Neither the boy nor the girl had any role to play, especially the latter. The parents' decision was "final". Even among the parents, men used to play a more decisive role.

There were times when the "selection" rule applied only to the girls, whereas the boys faced no such problems. The boys and their parents always had an upper hand.

All the probing and enquiries were confined to the girl's side only. Not only were pointed queries made about the girl's habits, but also how perfect she was in household chores, like cooking, embroidery, etc. At times, she was asked to cook to show her abilities. Though it was given to understand that the cooking had been done by the girl, some smart ladies from the boy's side could easily make out what sort of assistance she had received from others.

Exhibiting works of embroidery, supposed to have been done by the girl, was yet another way to impress the boy's parents and other elders. Colourfully embroidered 'good night', 'welcome', etc. on pillow covers and flowers, parrots, sparrows, peacocks on the bed covers were shown to them to convince them that the girl was very talented in the art of embroidery.

Then came times when 'seeing' and 'approving' of a girl (for the boys it came very late) became an 'essential' part of the matrimonial negotiations. Mostly these short girl-*dekho* sessions used to be held at the girl's place. The girl, attired in her best outfit, was asked to serve tea and snacks to the 'entourage' consisting of boy's parents, brothers and their wives, sisters and their husbands and some 'elders' who were considered experts in matrimonial matters, accompanying the boy. It was a 'feast' for all of them at the girl's parents expense, with no certainty that negotiations would ultimately 'succeed'.

As the ladies got busy in talking about the latest on 'fashion scene' or new jewellery designs or some other mundane topics, the menfolk engaged themselves probing and assessing the financial assets, especially of the girl's parents to get an 'approximate' idea how much dowry could be expected.

Though the boy used to take the liberty of snatching a glimpse of the girl, the latter sat with her head down. Even an occasional 'stolen' glance of the boy by the girl was considered unbecoming. This exercise used to be repeated a number of times till a suitable match was found for the girl. It used to be a very depressing exercise for the girl.

But it seems the times have changed altogether now. The girls and boys now prefer to hold these *dekho*-each-other-sessions in the lobbies of the hotels or five-star restaurants, depending on the status of the family, especially of the girl. But there are still some who are sticking to the old ways but not necessarily the 'meetings' take place at the girl's house. It could be the other way round also.

Now nobody talks about how versatile the girl is at cooking or embroidery. Rather casual enquiries are made whether the boy can afford a 'help' to assist the girl in household chores. Though the boy and the girl now talk about music and movies, the parents unfortunately still continue to evince interest in their respective moveable and immoveable properties and riches; all because dowry still plagues society. Incidentally, my nephew has decided to try his luck through the Internet. I wish him all the best.

81

KOTWAL UNCLE

Whenever I read about custodial deaths, I am reminded of my uncle who had served the police force during the British days. Both my uncle's father and grandfather had also served the police. But, unlike uncle, they could not rise beyond the rank of constable. Though Kotwal Uncle, as he was known, had also started as a constable, his heavy-handedness had pleased his seniors. With quick promotions, he rose to the rank of Kotwal.

Kotwal Uncle had evolved his own strategy of mend, bend and send to deal with criminals, dacoits, and other anti-social elements. Anyone brought to his kotwali would either mend himself, bend through confession or get eliminated (the code word for this was 'send') in case he refused to confess or fall in line. Hardcore criminals used to crack before him, and toughs used to quail at the thought being caned by him. Nobody ever questioned him, not even his seniors, about the methods he used to employ, as he faithfully served his duties so well.

His wife also used to enjoy the status of being known as the Kotwal's wife. The famous saying, *Saiyan bhaye kotwal ab darr kahe ka,* fit her like a glove. Everyday she would ride a tonga and go round the market, ordering everything and anything that caught her eye, without making payment. No shopkeeper dared ask her for payment. Rather they used to vie with each other to oblige Kotwal sahib's wife.

Then one day my aunt died of diarrhoea, leaving behind two teenaged sons. My uncle was at the police station squeezing a confession out of a young man arrested from his marriage *mandap* on suspicion of robbing an Englishman, a friend of the collector. As my uncle was under tremendous pressure to arrest the culprit, he glanced through the list of suspects in his area and arrested the young man, who could not stand uncle's caning and died in the lock-up. After his death, it was discovered to be a case of mistaken identity. Another notorious character with the same name was the culprit.

My uncle attributed the sudden death of my aunt to the young man's death and the curses of the girl he was to marry.

After my aunt's death, uncle was altogether a changed man. He got himself transferred to the police headquarters, where he was required to do only desk work. And then he broke the family tradition. He never allowed his two sons to join the police force.

82

SERVICE RULES

When some of my colleagues asked me to interact with the new boss till he settled down, I was half-inclined to undertake this thankless job. In fact, nobody wanted to be in his line of fire right from the beginning of his tenure.

He was known for his bad temper and bad mouth, accepting no suggestion and tolerating no criticism. No one was happy working with him. As a matter of fact, the staff of the department which he headed prior to his posting to our office, had distributed *prasad* on his departure.

Having accepted the responsibility of tackling the new boss, I evolved my own strategy.

Day one. I acquainted him with the working of the department. He was not a good listener. His restlessness showed it all.

Day two. I wanted him to meet the staff. "How silly of you. Do you expect me to meet a hundred persons by way of introduction?" I had a mind to tell him no one among the staff was keen to meet him either.

Day three. "When will your wife and children join you?" I asked. He was furious. "I am new to this place. I am still at company's guest house. I have yet to manage an accommodation".

"Don't worry, Sir", I assured him. "One of our colleague's father is a property dealer. He will manage everything for you". He looked pleased.

Day four. "What about your children's admission?" I enquired. "That is again a big problem", he replied. "Both my son and daughter are in high school".

Again I assured him that there was a gentleman in our department who would arrange admission for his children in any reputed school and without donation. The boss grinned.

Day five. "Sir you have not to worry about the ration card and transfer of your gas connection. We have a staffer who is an expert in getting such jobs done". The boss looked relaxed.

Day six. "Can you do me a favour?" the boss was somewhat indulgent. "Can you arrange for a cook at the guest house? My wife and children are arriving tomorrow".

"No problem, Sir. We have a daftary who is a very good cook. From tomorrow he will report at the guest house". The boss thanked me profusely.

The boss was no longer new. He had adjusted himself to the new office and the staff.

Thus was he kept in good humour all through his stay of a year and a half. The mundane mantras had worked out well.

83

GROOMING FOR THE GROOM

Finding a groom for your daughter is both an ordeal and an experience. Ordeal because you have to repeat, parrot-like, to whomsoever you meet the details about the girl, the family, jobs, assets, etc. However, the experience one gains from meeting strangers—many for the first and the last time—is really rewarding.

Not knowing who may turn out to be your *sambandhi*, you are very discreet—both in expression and action.

All the talk of a casteless society and advent into the computer age sounds meaningless when you find a large majority of the people stuck in the grooves of the caste system. The castes, sub-castes, regions, sub-regions, matching of the horoscopes (a *pandit* tells you matching is no problem), *gotras*, etc., continue to matter in matrimonial alliances. Even the most progressive are slavishly committed to all this.

Notwithstanding the propaganda against the dowry system on the small screen and through other media, the dowry-seekers (and also the dowry-givers who have ill-gotten money) are still ruling the roost. About a quarter of a century ago when I refused to accept any dowry I thought I was doing my bit for revolutionising our society. But when recently one of my nephews accepted a substantial sum at the time of *rokna* (the initial ceremony of fixing him up) I became firm in my view that dowry has become an inescapable part of the marriage ceremony.

One wonders why everybody wants only a slim, fair-complexioned; convent-educated (frankly speaking, I am not able to differentiate between a girl who has attended a convent school and another who has gone to a government school) girl, though the ladies around our homes are not worth much talking about.

The meaning of some of the terminology that is very often used while advertising for the bride become known to you only while you are looking for a match for your daughter.

The "highly-connected and status family" is the one which has fixed and mobile assets (without bothering to know how these were acquired), has close contacts with ministers, politicians, bureaucrats, etc. and can be exploited to the advantage of the groom. Such a family must be able to advance the business interests of the groom and his family.

"No demands" means "we will not object to what you give as dowry". "Simple marriage" means "do not ask the boy's side to spend anything". A "homely and accomplished" girl is the one who should be able to spend (even if she is working) much of her time in the kitchen while others watch the TV serials. "Girl's merits only consideration" means that she should have brains but should not use them!

Another interesting feature of matrimonial negotiations is the element of exaggeration in regard to the incomes and family backgrounds.

One fact that has emerged is that in India it is still a grooms' market and the girls and their parents take refuge under the umbrellas of *sanyog* (chance?) and luck.

They say marriages are made in heaven. But I feel, now human beings have taken the responsibility of making and unmaking them.

84

FULL CIRCLE

The old man came out of the park. He looked to the left, right, raised the stick he was carrying to let everyone know that he intended crossing the road. After reaching the middle of the road, he again looked towards the left and raised his stick. He had barely put his left foot forward when a speeding swanky car driven by a youngster came from a blind corner and hit him. The man fell down and was in awful pain.

The driver just rolled down the window pane and shouted, "You old hag, why do you come on the road if you cannot walk properly." Then he drove away, without caring to find out what injuries the man had suffered. I tried in vain to stop him from running away.

Another youngster who was also crossing the road and had seen the man being hit, ran towards him and waved a cycle-rickshaw to stop and with the help of the people who had gathered at the scene, put the man in the rickshaw and took him to a nearby clinic. I followed in another rickshaw.

Mercifully, there were no fractures, only some bruises. He was given first aid and an injection and allowed to go home. I offered to pay the doctor but the youngster insisted on doing so. "It is no big deal, uncle," he said.

The youngster and I took the injured man to his house. His family thanked us. "Only he deserves your thanks", I said pointing towards the youngster. "I wish the boy who hit him had also been like him." "No, uncle, I only did my duty," he said, somewhat modestly. "I know the boy who has hit him," the young samaritan added.

We decided to go to his house. The offending youngster was the son of a businessman. We told him about the hit-and-run accident. "So what do you want me to do?" asked the gentleman. His tone was rude, "Tell your son to be careful in future", I said.

The gentleman was offended. "What do you think he was driving a bullock cart?" We were shocked. How could a father who was supposed to be a role model for his son talk like this? As we were leaving, the son appeared on the scene, and said, "Why did the man come on the road unescorted?"

I had forgotten the incident when one morning while going through the newspaper I came across an obituary notice with a familiar face in the picture accompanying it. It was the youngster who had hit the old man.

I went to the house of the deceased to express my condolence. As the late youngster's father saw me, his lips quivered and tears started rolling down his cheek. I stood still, I couldn't even console him.

I was told the youngster met with an accident driving back from a party.

85

A HANDY MAN

Short of declaring me a good-for-nothing fellow, my wife has very often been critical of me for not being of much help in the household chores. And in a way she is quite justified.

Whether it is fixing of an electric fuse or setting right a leaking tap, I am always found wanting. I prefer calling an electrician or a plumber to do such jobs, which according to many require no expertise. At times I depend on an electrician for even replacing a fused bulb. Though many describe it a case of "pennywise and pound foolishness", to me it means just playing 'safe'.

The same is true with repairing a leaking tap. Even though I know that it requires only a replacement of a washer, I would ask a plumber to do the job. I am certain that if I try to open the tap either it will break or by the time I am able to replace the 'washer', the kitchen or the bathroom would get flooded. But the other day I really got offended when a plumber after repairing a leaking tap and taking a 'tenner', remarked 'I didn't know you couldn't even do this petty job.' Knowing my limitations, I took the remark in my stride.

Another job which frightens me is the ironing of the clothes. I have tried my hands many a time but failed. Either wrinkles or creases refuse to disappear or suddenly turn to 'black holes'. At best I can iron a 'hanky'.

My knowledge of cooking is limited to making a cup of tea. I know nothing, and have not tried to learn anything else, notwithstanding constant nagging of the betterhalf.

I sometimes feel bad when some hubbies proudly announce that they can cook. But frankly speaking I do not envy these 'great chefs' because I know at some point of time they might have been forced to learn cooking or trained by their wives to be 'standbys' in case of emergencies. But there are many other ways a husband can lighten up his wife's burden. I love doing dusting, sweeping and mopping the floors, when the maid suddenly takes off. Till recently I have been daily washing the car. Probably these small jobs are my saving grace. But I have one consolation. Till date nobody has dared to call me a 'h...husband'. You know what!

86

RESCUED BY A CARTMAN

Imagine my plight when my car suddenly broke down in the middle of a very busy road, very close to a crowded intersection during peak office hours, late in the evening. A thunderstorm was threatening any moment.

I was almost stuck in the car. The fast-moving vehicular traffic on both sides was making it difficult for me to come out of the car. Despite my putting the flashers on, nobody had the time to slow down his or her vehicle, leave aside stopping and helping me. Somehow or the other and taking a great risk, I came out of the car and waved at the drivers of the vehicles passing by but nobody bothered. Rather, they honked telling me to get aside.

With great difficulty I crossed the road and approached a traffic cop and sought his help.

"Sir, can you help me in pushing my car to a side?" I requested, intentionally using 'sir', to pamper his ego.

He gave me a furious look and said, "Can't you see I am the only one managing the traffic here?"

I had a mind to tell him that he was nowhere near to the point from where he was supposed to manage the traffic. Probably he was looking out for a big fish to earn extra bucks.

Seeing my plight, a roadside mechanic appeared from somewhere and offered to help me if I was ready to shell out 300 rupees. Being wary of roadside mechanics, I refused his help.

As I was making futile efforts to push my car, a *dhoti*-clad old man wearing a torn shirt suddenly appeared and offered to push the car.

He asked me to sit at the steering wheel as he single-handedly pushed the car to a safer place and started walking towards his handcart loaded with a washing machine and a television set.

I rushed after him and offered 50 rupees but he politely refused.

"*Meinne kuch nahin kiya, sahib ye to mera faraz tha,*" he said with a broad smile. I profusely thanked him and wished there could be many more like him around us.